Advance Praise for *The Solomon Syndrome*

"When we hired Bob as an associate producer on *The Bible Series,* we didn't know that we would become lifelong friends. Tapping into a half-century of biblical knowledge and personal experience, *The Solomon Syndrome* is a book every man or woman looking for a more meaningful life needs to read."

 —**Mark Burnett**, Producer of *The Voice*, *Survivor, Shark Tank, The Bible, AD: The Bible Continues*, *God, Chairman M⸱*   roup

                and

Roma Downey, actor,   .ers Media, Producer of *The Bible*   *.e Bible Continues, ...n of God,* and *Dovekeepers*

"I just read *The Solomon Syndrome*, right after contemplating my daily Proverb, a habit I picked up from the author. He lives this stuff. The book reads like a "Greatest Hits" of Bob's teaching, full of references to science, psychology, history, and pop-culture and Bob's most excellent gift, boiling down a biblical truth to its very essence and handing it off in a way anyone can understand. There is accessible wisdom on marriage, parenting, friendship, and personal growth to name a few. And if you take seriously the reflection questions (especially at the end of chapter one), your life will never be the same."

 —**David Meserve**, pastor, writer, faith entrepreneur, and Founder of UrbanSkye ministries in Denver, Colorado

"*The Solomon Syndrome* is an amazing guidebook for unlocking the secret to spiritual centeredness. I wish I had read it years ago!"

—**Frank Smith**, President and CEO of
Anschutz Film Group, Walden Media

"Have you ever hit a wall in your life? A broken relationship, a broken dream, or just a nagging feeling that something is not right? In *The Solomon Syndrome,* Bob creatively takes us on a journey to investigate why we put our hope in dreams and pursuits that were never supposed to fully satisfy. Johnny Lee's famous song about 'Lookin for love. . .' could easily have been titled 'Lookin for *Life* in all the Wrong Places.' Bob points us to secrets of the flourishing life for which we were each designed."

—**Doug Nuenke**, President of The Navigators, U.S.

"In a witty, logical, and quick-paced manner, Bob Beltz shows readers how to build new patterns for living to begin experiencing the spiritual riches Jesus promised. Bob Beltz captures your mind to challenge your emotional and spiritual moorings that reflect the choices shaping your life. I love Bob's honest approach to life's challenges, rooted in his convincing belief that our spiritual Father eagerly desires a full life for his children."

—**Luis Villereal**, Founder, Save Our Youth
in Denver, Colorado

"In the current age of unfettered materialism, Bob Beltz's study of Solomon—the world's wisest king, who nonetheless fell to his earthly desires—deserves a place in every believer's library."

—**Ben Warwick**, Founder and CEO, QES Investments,
Chief Investment Officer for Fort Point Capital Partners,
author of *Searching for Alpha*

"For over four decades, I have had the privilege of partnering with Bob Beltz in multiple ministries. I consider him one of my closest friends and one of the most gifted Bible teachers I have ever heard. *The Solomon Syndrome* grew out of years of retreats we did with men around the country, and to see these critically important concepts in print is thrilling. This is a book that can change your life.

—**Bo Mitchell**, Chaplain, Colorado Rockies, Founder and President of Crosswalk Fellowship Ministries, author of *Grace Behind Bars* and *Just Before Tip Off.*

"My friend, Bob Beltz, has written a very delightful and compelling book, *The Solomon Syndrome*. Bob has the gift you might say, even in the crucible of life, of finding patterns of humor and nuggets of truth that essentially make for a most satisfying read. In the midst of chapters with titles like "Boulevard of Broken Dreams," you will find other chapters titled, "Life's Too Short to Drive a Chevy" and "Transcending Nonconformity." Sustaining theology is witnessed throughout, along with searing and brutally honest life issues. A fulfilling read indeed."

—**Peb Jackson**, CEO, Jackson Consulting Group, Colorado Springs, CO

The Solomon Syndrome

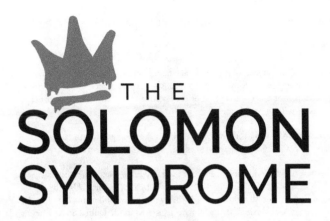

THE
SOLOMON
SYNDROME

A Blueprint for a More
Meaningful and Happy Life

DR. BOB BELTZ

NASHVILLE

NEW YORK • LONDON • MELBOURNE • VANCOUVER

THE **SOLOMON** SYNDROME

A Blueprint for a More Meaningful and Happy Life

Published in New York, New York, by Morgan James Publishing. Morgan James is a trademark of Morgan James, LLC. www.MorganJamesPublishing.com

Unless otherwise noted, Scriptures taken from the Holy Bible, New International Version®, NIV®.Copyright © 1973, 1978, 1984, 2011 by Biblica, Inc.™ Used by permission of Zondervan. All rights reserved worldwide. www.zondervan.com The "NIV" and "New International Version" are trademarks registered in the United States Patent and Trademark Office by Biblica, Inc.™

ISBN 9781631950445 paperback
ISBN 9781631950452 eBook
Library of Congress Control Number: 2020932340

Cover Design by:
Rachel Lopez
www.r2cdesign.com

Interior Design by:
Chris Treccani
www.3dogcreative.net

Morgan James is a proud partner of Habitat for Humanity Peninsula and Greater Williamsburg. Partners in building since 2006.

Get involved today! Visit
MorganJamesPublishing.com/giving-back

For Joy.
You have brought healing and
given me hope and a future.

Contents

Acknowledgments

would like to express my deep appreciation to the people who have made this book possible. First and foremost, I am grateful to Allison and my children, Stephanie and Baker, for providing the living laboratory in which the heart of this material has been field-tested over the years.

I am immensely grateful to my dear friend Bo Mitchell for inviting me to develop the material on relationships and priorities that we have taught together for over thirty years in our work with men and families.

I am deeply indebted to Dave Meserve, Biff Gore, Ken Lancaster, and the rest of the staff, elders, and members of Highline Community Church for the support and love they showed me during the difficult years of caring for Allison.

I am eternally indebted to Richard Beach who helped me break out of the Solomon Syndrome by introducing me to Jesus Christ.

And finally, thanks to the great team at Morgan James publishing for helping make the book available to a new generation and a new audience.

Preface

I t has been over twenty years since my book, *The Solomon Syndrome*, was first published by Fleming H. Revell Co. The book was a product of several years of speaking at retreats and churches on the subject of relationships. It also incorporated material I learned while working on my doctoral degree at Denver Seminary.

A great deal has changed since then. My children have grown up. My daughter and her husband have children of their own. After nearly fifty years of pastoral ministry, I have assumed the role of Pastor Emeritus of Highline Community Church. I am semi-retired even though I'm as busy as ever.

The greatest change has been the death of my wife, Allison, who plays a major role in the pages of this book. For seven years, I watched her fight a losing battle with Alzheimer's disease. For the first six of those years, I was her primary caregiver. On April 3, 2019, Allison went home to be with Jesus. He was the only man she loved more than me, and in the midst of the sorrow, I find great solace in her being with him.

I have written a number of books over the years. A number of them are now out of print. *The Solomon Syndrome* was one of them. I have started the process of updating and revising those that are no longer available to the general public. The book you have in your hands is one of them.

I have tried to live my life according to the principles contained in this book. I have no regrets. My hope is that you will find these words encouraging and challenging, and they will play a role in your spiritual journey.

September 4, 2019
Denver, Colorado

PART ONE

Beliefs, Boulevards, and Broken Dreams

A Guide to Assessment

CHAPTER ONE

Boulevard of Broken Dreams

(Understanding the Solomon Syndrome)

I n the times I needed a little emotional boost, I used to pack my wife and kids into the family car and head toward Gunther Toody's. Toody's was one of those trendy fifties-style diners where you could still get a big, greasy cheeseburger, fries, and a chocolate shake made with real ice cream. The waitresses all dressed in fifties garb while the jukebox cranked out an endless stream of golden oldies.

In the room where I liked to eat, a perfectly restored 1959 Corvette convertible hung from the ceiling and an eerie print adorned one wall. The print was a modification of a famous painting by Edward Hopper entitled *Nighthawks*. Painted in

1942, *Nighthawks* portrays a late-night scene at a lonely diner. Two men and a woman sit at the counter while another man waits on them behind it. In the Hopper painting, the occupants of the diner are unidentifiable.

German artist Gottfried Helnwein created the print at Gunther Toody's. Helnwein took the original Hopper painting and made a few changes. In the Helnwein version, we see the same late-night scene and the same diner, but now seated at the counter are James Dean, Humphrey Bogart, and Marilyn Monroe. Waiting on them behind the counter is none other than Elvis Presley. Helnwein entitled his work *Boulevard of Broken Dreams.*

I liked looking at the print with my wife and children nearby. It reminded me that even though I hadn't quite achieved the American Dream, maybe that dream wasn't all it was cracked up to be. What did these four celebrities have in common?

They all wanted to live full and happy lives. They wanted to feel good about themselves and about what they did. They all had dreams. They all pursued their dreams with passion. Unlike most men and women in the world today, these four achieved their dreams. In the end, however, the dreams ended up being broken dreams. All four died tragically, and in at least three cases, with great disillusionment.

I often found myself looking at the picture and asking the question, "What went wrong?" Why is it that so many of our dreams don't bring lasting happiness? The stories of the four people in the picture are certainly not unique.

The pages of history are filled with the accounts of men and women who appear to have lived lives of great success and yet were desperately unhappy. You would think we would get the message. Something is radically wrong! Our culture's definitions of the meaning of life and the way to be happy are defective. The path to happiness, contentment, fulfillment, and satisfaction is not the road of power, possessions, wealth, fame, and prestige. That road is usually a boulevard of broken dreams.

For some reason, it is very difficult to remember that the important things in life are often the things upon which our culture does not place great value. I am a rich man, though my bank account might not impress you. As I look at that Helnwein print, however, I am reminded of what is really important. I know what it takes to live in a way that offers an alternative to the despair and disillusionment represented by that work of art. There is a way of life that is characterized by a sense of harmony, contentment, and fulfillment. Discovering this new way requires a change in the way we look at life. This change begins by understanding the Solomon Syndrome.

Bad Theology

Ignatius J. Reilly is the central character in the Pulitzer prize-winning novel *A Confederacy of Dunces*. The book recently made the list of the one hundred favorite books highlighted in the PBS series *The Great American Read*. Riley is one of those off-center characters that march to the beat of a different drummer. In the opening chapter of the novel, Ignatius is standing in front of a department store observing the apparel of the men and women entering and departing. Spotting a woman dressed in a new and obviously expensive outfit, he makes the assessment that this is a person who lacks a sense of what Ignatius refers to as "good geometry and theology."

Ignatius himself is attired in an outfit that would best be described as "early Goodwill." His oversized corduroy slacks provide plenty of room for his even more oversized torso. His plaid flannel shirt and muffler shield his body so effectively that a coat is not required even though it is the dead of winter. The *piece de resistance* of the outfit is a bright red hunting cap, fully equipped with built-in earflaps; the earflaps are down, of course. The outfit reflects what Ignatius would classify as both good geometry and good theology.

In the world according to Ignatius J. Reilly, most problems are the result of bad theology (and geometry). Whether or not we would agree with the "theology" of *A Confederacy of Dunces*, one thing is clearly accurate about the observations made in the book: Bad theology can ruin your life.

Perhaps you have never realized that you have a personal theology. We all have belief systems that shape the decisions we make and steer the course of our lives. Your belief system is the foundation of your personal philosophy of life. These deeply ingrained convictions guide the choices, attitudes, and behaviors that shape your life. Your belief system is comprised of all the conscious and unconscious assumptions and beliefs you hold about how your personal needs are going to be met and what will make you happy.

We all know men and women who seem driven to make money. Our society is filled with people who appear to have this goal as their primary passion. If you could get inside that funny gray matter contained within their skulls, what would you find?

Later, I will go into some detail, describing the inner dynamics of the human motivational system. For now, let me simply state that such a money-driven person has exactly the same needs as you and me. His real needs are unconditional love and significance. Real needs are not always consciously known. They are often confused with what have been identified as felt needs. There is a critical difference between the two (which we will also explore in future chapters), but both are filtered through an internal set of beliefs about life and self.

Somewhere along the line, the money-driven person developed a belief system (perhaps not fully conscious) that the accumulation of money will meet his needs and make him happy. It is that basic assumption about how to get his needs met that has led to a lifestyle driven by the pursuit of money. Behavior is driven by belief, which in turn is rooted in needs.

In the coming chapters, I will show that our real needs are universally the same. Our beliefs and behaviors are as different as our individual experiences and convictions. Our behaviors are shaped by our goals, which are generated by our belief systems—our personal theology. Our behavior will produce outcomes that will either meet our deepest needs or fail to meet these needs. If our needs are met, our lives will be meaningful, fulfilling, and personally satisfying. If, on the other hand, the outcomes we achieve fail to meet our real needs, our lives will be frustrating, depressing, and filled with the vague sense that something is missing. A diagram of the above sequence would look like this:

Dynamics of Human Motivation

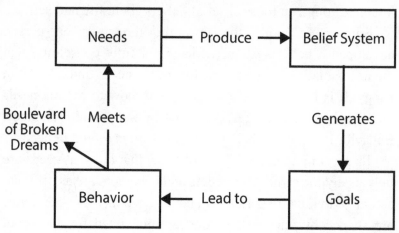

Faulty beliefs (bad theology) will lead to unfulfilling outcomes and unhappy lives! Most men and women in our society operate with defective belief systems. Our culture has effectively convinced them that some combination of wealth, power, prestige, and possessions will produce happiness, constituting what both Ignatius J. Reilly and Jesus Christ would call bad theology.

The Solomon Syndrome

Let's create a character much like one of the occupants of Helnwein's diner and attempt to answer that elusive question, "What went wrong?"

Think of a sweet little girl growing up in Southern California. By cultural standards, she is an exceptionally pretty little girl. All the attention and admiration she receives is based on her appearance. She receives false messages that will translate into her personal belief system as "Beauty earns security and significance." She becomes enamored with the lives of the men and women she sees on the silver screen at the local movie theater. She reads the manufactured stories of their glamorous lives reported in the movie magazines she buys at the corner drugstore. Her belief system begins to develop further: "Beauty can lead to fame. Fame can provide even more security and significance."

As her belief system continues to form, she gives no thought to the fact that what our culture defines as beauty fades and that fame is fleeting. She sees the nice cars and the extravagant homes of the rich and famous and adds another component to her belief system: "Fame leads to fortune. Fortune buys even more security and significance."

By the time she reaches young adulthood, her belief system is nearly intact. A photographer notices her beauty and offers to give her the first "break." In the midst of a normal photograph session, he convinces her to pose in the nude. Acquiescing, she might begin to experience the first costs of her faulty belief system; perhaps she feels used. Maybe she feels guilty. Unfortunately, the rapid acceleration toward fame and fortune produced by the photographs neutralizes those feelings, and the photographs open the door to a major studio screen test.

Let's fast-forward our story a bit. Fifteen or twenty years go by. Her beauty has been "enhanced" by bleached hair, expensive clothes, and a great deal of makeup. A change of name has accompanied the extraordinary fame she has experienced. Her fortune has allowed her to acquire anything money can buy. Her goals, based on her belief system have been fully realized. The critical question becomes, "Have her real needs been met?"

There is more to this picture than at first meets the eye. Since she never developed the ability to form lasting relationships based on a foundation other than her beauty, fame, and fortune, her life has been characterized by a string of painful, broken relationships. Fame and fortune cannot fill the void in her life, so she tries to anesthetize her pain with prescription drugs and alcohol. Yet, rather than easing the pain, her behavior only widens the void and increases the pain.

Finally, the staggering reality of aging begins to set in. Wrinkles begin to appear. She begins to gain weight. Sleepless nights and alcohol-induced stupors take their toll. The foundations of her belief system are crumbling. In one final act of desperation she ends her life with an overdose of sleeping pills. Good-bye, Norma Jean!

Norma Jean Mortenson, better known as Marilyn Monroe, was a classic victim of what I call the Solomon Syndrome. It is one of the most prevalent philosophies of life in our world today. It always, ultimately, leads a person down the Boulevard of Broken Dreams. It is a philosophy of life as old as civilization itself. I call it the Solomon Syndrome because it was never more perfectly expressed than in the life of the third king of the United Kingdom of Israel.

Much of what God attempts to accomplish by giving us a written record of the redemptive history of his people is the impartation of a bit of perspective. This is one of the primary reasons God preserved a piece of the life and teaching of the man named Solomon.

Solomon is a perfect example of what happens when a man or woman loses perspective and deviates from the divine blueprint. Alternatives to the blueprint can be incredibly appealing. A good friend of mine coined the expression "the world's menu" to capture the appeal of the multitude of choices we face each and every day of our lives.

It used to be relatively easy to order lunch at McDonald's. You either ate a hamburger, a cheeseburger, or a fish sandwich.

McDonald's has added more items to the menu, so it takes a bit more thought now. When you eat at a more sophisticated restaurant you often face a dizzying multitude of choices.

Life in our culture offers an incredibly diverse "menu." As a result, the quality of perspective becomes even more crucial. Without an accurate perspective on life, we can spend years pursuing choices on the menu that simply aren't fulfilling. Solomon has much to teach us in this regard.

Solomon was the son of King David. When David turned the throne of Israel over to him, the nation was at the beginning of its Golden Age. Solomon ruled Israel for forty years. They were years of peace and prosperity for the nation of Israel and for Solomon.

Solomon was a man who had everything going for him. Yet at the height of his career, Solomon "hit the wall." From his unique vantage point he wrote a personal reflection on the detours and dead-ends of life. This short reflection is preserved for us in the Bible under the book title Ecclesiastes.

Power

In this short book, Solomon makes a series of statements regarding his accomplishments. He follows each statement with an assessment of the accomplishment. He begins the treatise with the statement that he is the king in Jerusalem. (Eccles. 1:1) This was a man who possessed great political power. We live in a world that teaches us that power will give our lives significance. There is perhaps no greater symbol of power than the throne of a monarch. Solomon occupied such a throne at the pinnacle of his nation's glory.

He wielded power over the lives and affairs of men and nations. Many men and women have lived and died in the pursuit of this kind of power. Even today, people will go to almost any sacrifice and expense to gain public office so they might exercise political power. For many, this quest has purely altruistic motives. But the biographies of power-hungry people often lead one to believe that this drive for power is often rooted in a man or woman's basic need for significance. The quest for power becomes an attempt to satisfy a need. Is it possible to satisfy this need with political, economic, or military power? Let's look at Solomon's assessment of his situation.

The Solomon Syndrome

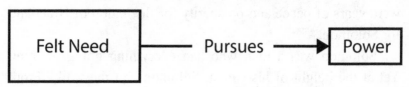

In the opening statement of Ecclesiastes, Solomon makes a rather dismal assessment of the state of his emotional life. His often-repeated formula reads, "Vanity of vanities; all is vanity." (Eccles. 1:2, KJV) I like the way the New International Version translates it: "Meaningless! Meaningless! . . . Utterly meaningless! Everything is meaningless." Solomon's message is clear: Even if we reach the pinnacles of power our lives will not be fulfilled if power is an end in and of itself.

Pleasure

Solomon's position enabled him to pursue another path in his quest for personal fulfillment. When power didn't do it, he became a hedonist. His belief system shifted to: "Eat, drink, and be merry." Solomon was quite a modern man in this regard. The main difference between Solomon and Joe Cool at the local single's bar is that Solomon had the ability to pursue pleasure in a way, and to a degree, that few of us could ever match.

The Solomon Syndrome

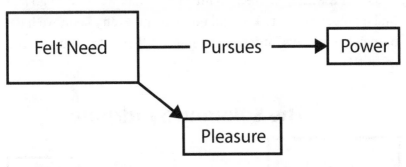

Solomon could honestly say, "I denied myself nothing my eyes desired." (Eccles. 2:10) He tested his heart with pleasure, filled his belly with wine, and kept a harem of three hundred concubines to meet his sexual desires when his seven hundred wives bored him. This was a guy who understood the meaning of the adage "wine, women, and song!"

What was his assessment of this pursuit? "Everything was meaningless, a chasing after the wind." (Eccles. 2:11) Pleasure did not fill the void created by the deep need for love and meaning. "Fun" can numb the pain for a while, but it is not a lasting solution to the quest for personal fulfillment.

Possessions

When power and pleasure don't fill the void, what do you turn to next? For Solomon, it was possessions. George Carlin, the irreverent comedian and astute observer of human behavior, loved to talk about our culture's obsession with "stuff." Carlin pointed out that at some time in our lives we all start out with very little stuff. As we grow older, we have the tendency to begin to accumulate stuff. Pretty soon, we have so much stuff that we have to build a house. What is a house? It is a place where you keep your stuff! Sometimes, after we have lived in a house for a while, we have so much stuff that we have to go and find a bigger house to keep all our stuff in. Pretty soon we have basements, closets, attics, and garages filled with, you guessed it, stuff!

The Solomon Syndrome

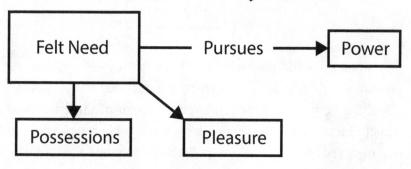

I remember when I graduated from college and left home to begin my first job. I drove a little yellow Volkswagen beetle in those days. All my "stuff" fit right in my car. After a few years away from home, I met my wife, Allison. We got married. That's when you really begin to accumulate stuff! We spent the first years of married life living in the middle of Nebraska. On weekends, our favorite activity was to go to farm auctions. An auction, of course, is a place where you can buy stuff other people don't have room for any more. When we finally moved from our first little house and went to another job in another city, we still had a little Volkswagen. But this time, we had to pull a trailer behind it to move all our stuff. The next time we moved, it took a truck to move our stuff. On our last move, we needed to make two trips with the truck. We have really accumulated a lot of stuff!

As much stuff as we have, it fades in comparison with Solomon's stuff. He had palaces, stables, gardens, parks, and storehouses filled with stuff. He owned flocks, slaves, chariots, and all kinds of great stuff. Did it satisfy his deepest needs? Once again his assessment of the situation was "meaningless." (Eccles. 2:11)

Wealth

If there is one predominant message men and women in Western culture have adopted as part of their belief system, it is that money makes us happy. Solomon was a man who amassed great wealth. There are several passages in the Old Testament that give us information regarding Solomon's wealth. One day, I began to calculate his annual income. As I put these pieces together, I discovered that Solomon's annual income was somewhere, conservatively speaking, in the range of several billion dollars a year, tax free. In 1000 B.C., that kind of cash went a long way! That flow of income continued for over forty years, giving Solomon a mind-boggling net worth, not even counting his real estate holdings. In today's standards, his wealth would be incalculable. By all standards, he was the wealthiest man on the face of the earth. Here is his assessment of his wealth:

> *"Whoever loves money never has money enough;*
> *whoever loves wealth is never satisfied with his income.*
> *This too is meaningless."*
>
> (Eccles. 5:10)

When our life is built around the pursuit of money, the end will certainly be frustration. Part of the tragedy of this pursuit lies in the fact that by the time we figure out its futility, it is often too late to concentrate on the things that truly give meaning and purpose to life. The cost of the pursuit of wealth is often found in the destruction of the relationships that really do matter.

The Solomon Syndrome

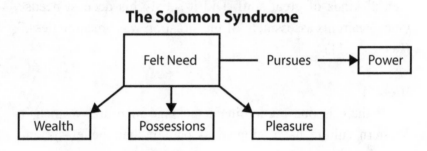

Education

We also live in a society preoccupied with information. Some humanists believe the ultimate destiny of mankind hinges on technology and the education of the global village. They think the answers to the dilemmas that face humanity are locked away in the human brain, waiting to be freed by the educational process or the development of artificial intelligence. Yet in the most highly educated society in human history, many of the most highly educated people are the most miserable.

Solomon was no exception. In addition to being powerful and wealthy, he was brilliant. In his early years, before he experienced the disillusionment reflected in Ecclesiastes, Solomon had a marvelous encounter with God. One night God appeared to him and offered him an envious opportunity: "Ask for whatever you want me to give you." (2 Chron. 1:7)

In one of those rare moments of clarity that seem to come too infrequently in life, Solomon made a request reflecting a completely unselfish motivation.

"Give me wisdom and knowledge," he said, "that I may lead this people, for who is able to govern this great people of yours?" (2 Chron. 1:10)

The Solomon Syndrome

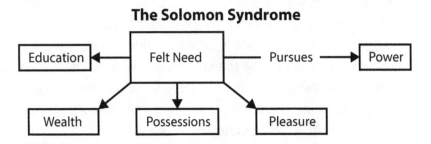

God was pleased with Solomon's request. He not only granted the request, he added to it wealth, honor, and riches. (2 Chron. 1:12) Solomon's intellectual capabilities became world famous. People from all over the known world traveled to Jerusalem just to listen to the wisdom of Solomon. If education were the key to personal fulfillment, Solomon would have been a very happy man. Yet, when we look at his assessment of his great wisdom we read, "What then do I gain by being wise? . . . This too is meaningless." (Eccles. 2:15)

Think about it! Every element of the belief system advocated by contemporary culture as the pathway to the good life was fully achieved and experienced by this man. He accomplished the goals of which most people only dream. What did he find? He discovered that for years, he had been traveling down the Boulevard of Broken Dreams. The achievement of his goals produced nothing but futility. His real needs were not met.

How many people do you know who are trapped in the Solomon Syndrome? Multitudes of men and women will spend the limited years of their lives pursuing goals that will never meet their needs.

At the end of his reflection, Solomon drew a couple of poignant conclusions about escaping this syndrome. The last chapter of Ecclesiastes begins with his advice to "Remember your Creator in the days of your youth." (Eccles. 12:1) We could paraphrase this advice by affirming that real meaning and purpose in life will only be found in a spiritual solution to life's challenges. Solomon concludes his discourse by saying, "Now all has been heard; here is the conclusion of the matter: Fear God and keep his commandments." (Eccles. 12:13)

How can you break out of the Solomon Syndrome? Let Solomon himself tell you: Assess and adjust! Through Solomon, we are challenged to reevaluate our belief systems and the behaviors generated by our philosophy of life. Do we have some bad theology? If we reached our goals, would they bring the fulfillment that meeting our deep needs for security and significance brings?

If you realize that you are trapped in the Solomon Syndrome, you can change. Faulty belief systems can be replaced. It will require some work on your part.

In the following chapters I am going to take you on an inward adventure. I hope to help you understand how you got trapped in the syndrome and how to make the necessary changes to your "geometry and theology" that will keep you off the Boulevard of Broken Dreams and move you into a way of living that leads to fulfillment and true happiness.

Personal Reflection

In the coming chapters, I will show you how to take some specific steps to break out of the Solomon Syndrome. Before you move on, you might find it helpful to stop and think about a few questions:

- What are some of your basic assumptions about life?
- How much of your current belief system is faulty?
- In what ways are you caught up in the Solomon Syndrome?
- Do you want God's best for your life?
- Are you willing to change?

CHAPTER TWO

Life's Too Short to Drive a Chevy

(and Other Guidelines for Intentional Living)

A number of years ago, I saw a T-shirt that captured my attention. It sported the Porsche logo in large bold letters across the front of the shirt. Underneath the logo, in freestyle lettering, the shirt declared, "Life's too short to drive a Chevy." Don't get me wrong. I have nothing against Chevrolets or any other make of car. But as a car enthusiast, I knew exactly what the creator of the shirt was attempting to communicate.

The shirt was more of a statement about one's philosophy of life than a critique of General Motors. Many people go through life driving Chevrolets and are perfectly content. Others negotiate the years harboring a secret desire to own a vehicle like a Porsche. They find themselves experiencing sensations of envy every time they pull up to a stoplight next to some sharp, little masterpiece of German engineering. In the back of their minds, they are always thinking, "Someday, I'll own one of those." It just seems like that elusive "someday" never arrives.

Life is like that. Life is short. As a matter of fact, life is too short. Too short to drive a Chevy? Maybe, if a Chevy becomes the symbol of missing all the gusto. It is certainly too short to allow many of the really important issues of life to slide by. How can we be sure we don't miss the precious gifts life has to offer? What are the areas of life that deserve our concentration and effort? What makes life worth living? What gives life purpose and meaning? How can we make the adjustments necessary to get more out of life?

Intentional Living

A few years ago, John Denver recorded a clever little song about making radical changes in your life. In the chorus of the song, Denver encouraged listeners to blow up their TVs, throw away their newspapers, and move to the country.

The song had a special appeal to people who longed to escape the rat race. It reminded us that life is too short to live in bondage to a lifestyle that can never deliver what it promises. Many people live in bondage, and some even recognize that they are in bondage. Few know how to get free.

There are two radically different approaches to living. One is manipulated living, characterized by the man who does not have control over his life. The term "rat race" is often used to describe this way of living. People whose lives are manipulated seldom experience a great deal of personal fulfillment. What they usually experience is a kind of bondage.

The other style of living is more intentional. Intentional living is making conscious choices about the way we live; it is usually based on certain principles or values. A man who is living intentionally will either be found leading the race or refusing to run; he has a sense that he is in control of his destiny. If we are going to experience life in all its fullness, we must learn to live intentionally. We must also have the correct set of values and principles as the basis of our intentionality.

Both manipulated living and intentional living are products of the same series of dynamics that are basic to all human behavior. Our behavior is the product of the choices we make about how we will live. The sum of these choices creates our lifestyle. Adjustment is the process whereby an individual intentionally makes a series of choices and undertakes a plan of action to redefine and reshape his or her lifestyle.

The adjustment process begins by clarifying the underlying needs that motivate our behavior. We respond to our needs, as we understand them, by adopting certain beliefs about how our needs will be met. In the previous chapter we identified the fact that many of us have adopted belief systems that are in need of radical change. Our belief systems are manifested in a series of choices and actions designed to pursue the goals, which we believe will lead to the fulfillment of our felt needs. The outcomes of our choices and behavior determine our existing lifestyles.

To move to a more intentional lifestyle, we must be able to identify the structure that is already in place. Our lifestyles are made up of three primary building blocks. We each have a certain amount of time, energy, and money to invest in the choices we make about how we will live our lives. An analysis of these resources will reveal what our existing life structure looks like. It is this life structure that actually identifies our philosophy of life.

If you were to ask about my philosophy of life, I could easily articulate a sequence of relational priorities to which I am committed. Conceptually, I have my life well ordered. Pragmatically, I have a bit of a problem living out what I have developed conceptually. If you want to know about my real philosophy of life, simply evaluate the percentage of my primary resources I invest in those different areas of priority.

Evaluating the use of my resources will also reveal the extent to which I am living intentionally (versus manipulatively). The amount of discrepancy between those things I say are my priorities and my investment of time, energy, and money reveals the extent to which I operate under manipulation.

Later in this book, I will explore the spiritual dimension of life. Even if my resources are invested consistently with my priorities, I will still need to determine whether the priorities of my life fit with the priority structure God designed. The two questions each of us must face in making assessments and adjustments are: (1) Am I in bondage to a lifestyle that is running me? and (2) Am I intentionally creating a lifestyle that is out of harmony with God's best for my life?

Someday, I will have to make a decision. Has the pursuit of my goals met the deep needs of my life? Do I feel good about my life and myself as a result of the belief system I have followed, the values I have adopted, and the choices I have made? The answer to these questions can mark the beginning of a major transition time in our lives.

Students of human behavior have discovered that these periods of evaluation and transition often lead to times of crisis in the adult life cycle. An unsatisfactory evaluation can lead to changes in career, marriage, geography, or something else in an attempt to get needs met. Without an accompanying change in our belief system, these transitions become no more than brief detours that ultimately lead back to the Boulevard of Broken Dreams. After a series of these transitions, life begins to wind down and we are suddenly faced with the fact that life is too short and somehow we have wasted it. But that need not be the case.

"Protest Against the Rising Tide of Conformity"

Change is difficult. We tend to lock into behavior patterns that become habits. Often these habits and the belief systems that lie behind them are extremely complex in their origins. They are a product of the constant bombardment of the Zeitgeist (spirit of the age) and the dynamics of personality development that have shaped our lives. When these dynamics lead us to buy into the prevailing value system of the culture and respond with corresponding behavior, we become locked into conformity.

A number of years ago, I decided it was time for a new family photo. We had not had one taken in several years, and I wanted to do something a little different. A good friend of mine, Ken Bisio, is a well-known professional photographer. His work hangs in some of the better galleries in the States and abroad. I called Ken and asked if he would "shoot" our family in a kind of funky family photo. Ken told me he knew just the spot and directed us to meet him at an abandoned warehouse in lower downtown Denver, an area known locally as "Lo-Do."

Our whole family dressed in our motorcycle gear and headed for Lo-Do. My wife, Ali, and daughter, Stephanie, drove the car while my son, Baker, and I rode my Harley. When we arrived at the warehouse we immediately knew why Ken picked that particular spot. Spray-painted on the warehouse door was the graffiti challenge, "Protest Against the Rising Tide of Conformity." We all assumed a Harley attitude and Ken captured the scene on Kodachrome. The "family portrait" came out great.

The message painted on that warehouse door is a critical one for many men and women in America. The time has come to protest against conformity to a defective cultural belief system; it is time to break out of a manipulated lifestyle, to reverse the Solomon Syndrome. The big question becomes, "How do we do it?"

Nearly two thousand years ago, a man named Jesus gave a formula for making the break. "You will know the truth, and the truth will set you free." (John 8:32) These words of Jesus contain a formula for breaking out of bondage and moving into a life of freedom. Jesus Christ is a liberator. He liberates in a multitude of ways. One of the more exciting ways he liberates is in this area of breaking free from defective belief systems and unfulfilling lifestyles.

The formula was preceded by a condition, a prerequisite for experiencing the liberating power of Jesus. "If you hold to my teaching," Jesus said, "you are really my disciples." (John 8:31) The prerequisite for freedom is a willingness to change. We must recognize that our definition of our needs and our belief system about how they will be met might be faulty. This is not easy because it requires what the Bible calls humility. Our natural tendency is to justify and rationalize our lives. By nature, we are more prideful and stubborn than humble. Openness to change is a big step in the right direction.

Once we have taken the step of openness to change, we must be willing to accept a new source of authority. Jesus also made a bold statement about those who would be willing to model their lives around his teaching. He said, "I have come that you might have life, and have it to the full." (John 10:10) That statement is either true or false. If it is false, then Jesus was a fraud. If it is true, we would be wise to rethink life from the perspective of his teachings.

If we are going to experience true liberty our new authority on life must now become the author of life himself. We need to find out if God has anything to say about our needs and how to meet them. His revealed truth needs to become the basis of our belief system. We must then attempt to develop life goals that are consistent with what we discover.

Finally, having accepted a new source of authority, we commit ourselves to choices and behaviors that are in harmony with our new belief system. When these commitments have been put into practice we should begin to experience the fulfillment of Jesus' life-changing promise. We will know the truth, and applying the truth will set us free from our ineffective patterns of thinking and living.

The truth challenges our personal theology and reveals which parts of our belief systems are faulty. Here are a few "truths" that should affect our approach to living:

> 1. *We are going to die.* You have probably heard the expression, He who dies with the most toys wins. I have a t-shirt that corrects this statement. Mine says: He who dies with the most toys still dies!
>
> One of the greatest men in human history wrote, "Teach us to number our days aright, that we may gain a heart of wisdom." (Ps. 90:12) His name was Moses. To "number one's days aright" is to come to grips with the reality that life is short and one day we are going to die. In the book of Genesis, we read that God told Adam the violation of his prohibition would lead to death. (Gen. 2:17) The Devil, in the form of a serpent, told Eve that she would not die. This lie, which led to the temptation and fall of humanity, was a denial of death. Pragmatically, many men still live as if this lie were true. It is not. The truth is, you and I are going to die.
>
> 2. *This world is going to pass away and a new world is coming.* It seems that even those who claim to believe this truth find it difficult to believe it in a way that changes their behavior.

The world in which we live is in a state of progressive deterioration. The final destiny of this world is disintegration and destruction. But, there is a new world coming—a world that is lasting and eternal. You and I can experience a "preview" of this coming world by tapping into the divine blueprint now.

3. *The things of this world will never meet our real needs.* Our motto in this regard should be "Remember Solomon!" Solomon learned that everything the world has to offer produces only frustration, despair, and emptiness. In the chapters that follow, I hope to demonstrate the solution to breaking out of the Solomon Syndrome is found in a relational network God designed to meet our deepest needs. Only loving relationships, cultivated with a serving attitude and characterized by authentic spirituality, will meet our real needs.

Jesus said freedom would be the result of knowing the truth. The truth gives us "magic eyes" that allow us to see life from a different perspective. If we are going to break out of the Solomon Syndrome, we must cultivate perspective. Perspective generates an awareness that enables us to structure our lives with a sense of divinely ordained priority.

Jesus lived a totally free and full life. There was not one trace of bondage in his life. He lived the most satisfying and significant life in all of human history. We often forget that the knowledge, power, and resources to live any way he desired were at his disposal. If those same resources were available to you and me, we might have chosen a lifestyle much like Solomon's. But Jesus lived a life heavily invested in relationships instead of "stuff."

He loved and he served. He lived in harmony with the truth, absolutely free and full of joy. He was perfectly fulfilled. He is our model of what living well really looks like. In order for you and me to live the same way, we probably need to make a few adjustments. Let's begin by seeing how to gain a quality of perspective that motivates us to become unwilling to settle for less in life than God's best!

Personal Reflection

Perhaps you have never given much thought to the idea of manipulated living. Here are a few questions to think about that might help you assess your own life.

- Do you feel free?
- How are you trapped in the "rat race"?
- What is important to you?
- How does the use of your primary resources reflect the above priorities?

CHAPTER THREE

The World According to Tripper Harrison

(The Need for Perspective)

The word *paradigm* is often used these days to refer to a person's frame of reference. Stephen R. Covey, who popularized the word in his book, *The Seven Habits of Highly Effective People*, says that a paradigm is "the way we see the world." A paradigm functions as a mental map that provides direction as we travel the road of life. In order for change to occur in our lives it is often necessary to experience what Covey calls a paradigm shift. A paradigm shift requires a change in our philosophy of life. It demands fresh perspective and a new set of priorities to govern our life decisions. To live according to a belief system that goes against the grain of popular culture requires frequent times of appraisal and adjustment. It means a man needs to cultivate a perspective of life that is linked to a set of priorities, which enable him to live sanely in what often feels like an insane world.

Over the last twenty years, I've served as a consultant and associate producer on over thirty Hollywood films. I find that even in some mediocre films, there is often a scene that makes watching the entire movie worthwhile. Such is the case with one of my favorite movies, *Meatballs.*

The movie is the story of an odd assortment of characters who share a summer together at Camp Northstar. The highlight (or lowlight, depending on how you look at it) of the summer is a weekend of competition that takes place between the young men and women of Camp Northstar and their archrivals from Camp Mohawk.

To fully appreciate the scene, you need to understand something about these two camps. The head counselor of Camp Northstar is a character by the name of Tripper Harrison, played by comedian Bill Murray. It would be an understatement to say that Tripper marches to the beat of a different drummer. Tripper describes Northstar as "the best camping experience available . . . in this price range." Most of the kids who come to spend a summer at Northstar are there because they can't afford to go anywhere else.

Across the lake sits Camp Mohawk, where no expense has been spared in either design or construction. Nor has any expense been spared by the parents of the children who are sent each summer to Camp Mohawk. Every year for the last twelve years, the campers of Camp Mohawk have crushed the Camp Northstar campers in the end-of-summer competition.

The scene that grabbed me takes place after the first day of competition in this annual rivalry. Northstar is once again getting creamed. It is evening and the campers from Northstar are sitting around the fireplace, completely dejected. In the midst of their dejection, Tripper stands to speak. His discourse, as I remember it, runs something like this:

"I know what you're thinking," Tripper begins. "For twelve years we've been beaten by these guys. But, you know, it just doesn't matter." The volume of Tripper's voice slowly begins to increase. "Sure, they have the best athletes and the best equipment money can buy, but it just doesn't matter." (The campers, still dejected, begin to look up at Tripper.)

"I know, they have the most sophisticated training programs borrowed from the U.S.S.R., and they have their blood and urine tested daily." (The campers begin to come to life as the volume of Tripper's voice continues to increase.) "But it just doesn't matter!"

"Sure, they use the latest performance-enhancing drugs, but it just doesn't matter." At this point, Tripper is almost shouting.

"And even if we were to win, if we were to perform so far over our heads that our noses began to bleed, and if God in heaven were to smile on every man, woman, and child among us, it just doesn't matter!" (The campers are now totally enthralled and on the edge of their seats.) "Because all the really good-looking girls would still go out with their guys, because they have all the money! It just doesn't matter!"

At this point Tripper begins to lead the entire group as they stand and chant together, "It just doesn't matter! It just doesn't matter! It just doesn't matter!" Of course, as always happens in the movies, with their newfound sense of perspective, the Northstar campers go out the next day and win the competition.

The scene had a rather strange effect on me. For the next few days, those words, "It just doesn't matter," kept floating through my mind at the most interesting times. I got up in the morning, looked in the mirror at my balding head, and thought, "It just doesn't matter." I sat at a stoplight and someone pulled up next to me in some fine piece of automotive engineering that would normally evoke all manner of covetousness, and a voice inside my head reminded me, "It just doesn't matter!"

The following weekend, my wife and I went out to dinner with several couples. One of the women in the group, a fashion consultant, delivered a monologue on the critical importance of what we wear. As I intently maintained the proper communication skills of eye contact, mixed with slight affirmative head nod, little could she know that the words floating through my mind were "It just doesn't matter!" Don't get me wrong. All those things (hair, cars, and clothes) are nice. But in the big picture of life, they really don't matter all that much.

"It just doesn't matter!" Some critics have said it is the most demotivating speech in human history. I disagree. Those might be the four most important words in the English language when arranged in that order. They reflect a sense of perspective that is critical if we are to live effectively. Perspective is a critical component of our internal belief system. I'm convinced that every man and woman on the planet (or at least in our culture) is searching for a life that is personally fulfilling and satisfying. I have never met or counseled a man or woman who, at the core of their motivational system, was not engaged in this pursuit.

Unfortunately for many, the pursuit seems as futile as Northstar's attempts to defeat Mohawk. It seems tragic that many men and women live lives, as Thoreau said, of "quiet desperation" when their hearts long for personal fulfillment.

They accomplish little but frustration and despair. For many, one factor producing this futility is the inability to know when to apply these four little words: "It just doesn't matter!"

Failure to achieve fulfillment also involves the "flip side" of these words, that is, the inability to discern and pursue those objectives and goals that really do matter. There is a belief system that will help you answer the question, "What really matters?"

At the simplest possible level, the answer is *You* matter! Your life is important. You were created to live a full and meaningful life. You were created to live with a God-given sense of significance. Your life has a purpose. There is an approach to life that will maximize the joy of living. You really matter!

Not only do you matter, but other people matter. You are surrounded by a network of relationships, which are designed to make your life full and meaningful. Relationships really matter. In our frantic pursuit of happiness, we often rush by the real sources of joy in life. We need to understand the design of the universe and how relationships play a central role in that design.

Finally, it is important to know that God really matters. Maybe you don't think of yourself as a religious person; neither do I. Religion is not what really matters. What really matters is a relationship with God that provides us with a spiritual solution to life's challenges. These are the realities that give life meaning and joy. There is a purposeful plan to life that works. Many men and women have never discovered this truth. When issues of meaning and significance are addressed, they feel a great deal like Arthur Dent.

The Hitchhiker's Guide to the Three-Dimensional Man

How would you feel if you awoke one morning and discovered that in exactly twelve minutes, Earth was going to be destroyed? Such was the case for Arthur Dent in Douglas Adam's classic book, *The Hitchhiker's Guide to the Galaxy*. It is the first in a trilogy of books written by Adams that explores the "big questions" of the meaning of life in a somewhat offbeat manner.

In the trilogy, Arthur Dent and his friend Ford Prefect (who turns out to be a roving reporter for an electronic, cosmic publication called *The Hitchhiker's Guide to the Galaxy*) escape the destruction of our planet by hitching a ride on a passing spaceship called the "Heart of Gold." During the course of their adventures Arthur discovers the Earth is actually an artificial planet created to run an organic computer program. In the books, we discover that a race of highly intelligent, pan-dimensional beings designed a computer millions of years ago to answer the question, "What is the meaning of life?" After processing for decades, the computer finally arrived at the answer: "Forty-two."

The highly intelligent beings were perplexed, to say the least. Upon further inquiry, the computer went on to inform these beings that the answer was meaningless without knowing the right question. Earth was then built to produce "The Question." (If all of this seems a bit bizarre, let me assure you it is! But stick with me for a moment.)

At the end of the second book in the trilogy, Arthur and Ford discover "The Question" that fits "The Answer" and theoretically explains the meaning of life. In a random drawing of letters from a prehistoric word game, the question is formed: "What do you get if you multiply six by nine?" Forty-two? In the BBC production of the trilogy, Arthur comments, "I always knew there was something fundamentally wrong with the universe."

In the final pages of the trilogy, it is revealed to Arthur that the question and the answer to the meaning of life are mutually exclusive. Knowledge of one, Arthur is told, logically precludes knowledge of the other. Now, what is the significance of all this insanity? The humorous but tragic message of Mr. Adams's books is the ultimate meaning of life can never be known. The underlying philosophical presupposition of *The Hitchhiker's Guide to the Galaxy* is we are all victims of a mass, cosmic, practical joke.

I should point out that although Adams's books are humorous and entertaining, Adams himself was an outspoken atheist. His conclusions are not that uncommon in the world today. Many people in our world feel like they are lost in space. One distinctive that sets humanity apart from every other species on the planet is an inborn quest for a sense of meaning and purpose. It is as if our genetic code contains a desire to know what life is all about. We have been designed to live fully only when we are able to discover a sense of meaning and purpose. Without such a sense, people are destined to waste their years either living "lives of quiet desperation," or more likely, lives of frantic futility. It need not be so. It is possible to know both the question and the answer.

Three-Dimensional Man

There is a divine design in the universe. Your life has a purpose. You can live with a sense of meaning. God has designed a system. When our lives are brought into conformity with this system, we will begin to live in a more meaningful and significant way.

To borrow a phrase from the late philosopher and theologian Francis Schaeffer, "He is there, and He is not silent." God is alive, not dead, and he has spoken. There is a divine blueprint for life. The first words of that majestic piece of literature we call the Bible is the statement, "In the beginning God created the heavens and the earth." (Gen.1:1) The God of the Bible is the architect and designer of the universe. In the Bible, you can discover how he designed the cosmos to operate and what has gone wrong with his design. By understanding what "the book" has to say about these things, we will take the first steps toward developing perspective in our lives.

The blueprint is threefold. First, it tells us who we were intended to be. Second, it explains what makes us tick. Third, it describes how we are to live. When you put these three pieces of the puzzle together, you will have "the big picture" of how God designed your life to have meaning and purpose. Each of the next three chapters will deal with one dynamic of this blueprint.

The Physical Dimension

God is infinite; God is personal. With perfect knowledge, wisdom, power, and love, God chose to create the physical universe. The crowning touch of God's creation was a creature designed to reflect his very image. "God said, 'Let us make man in our image.'" (Gen. 1:26) The creation of humanity in the image of God makes it possible for men and women to live in a meaningful relationship with God himself.

Many of us have been taught that we are nothing more than physical beings. This materialistic view of life leaves little room for any meaningful definition of existence. The materialist's formula for explaining life looks something like this:

TIME + CHANCE + MATTER = LIFE

In contrast to this definition, the second chapter of the book of Genesis gives a brief synopsis of human origins from a spiritual perspective. Verse 7 of that chapter affirms the truth that men are physical beings. We read, "God formed the man from the dust of the ground." (Gen. 2:7) However, as the text continues we find that man is much more than a one-dimensional physical being.

As physical beings, we are partially composed of matter, fashioned into material bodies, which live in contact with the physical world. We experience the physical world through the senses God created. We are able to see, touch, taste, hear, and smell. We have the capacity to experience physical pain and pleasure. These characteristics of our lives are part of the divine design and have been given the divine seal of approval. God said, "It is good!" But you and I are much more than mere physical creatures.

The Psychological Dimension

Genesis 2:7 tells us that God created us to become "living beings." The Hebrew word "being" in this passage is often translated by using the English word "soul." This is the primary word used in the Old Testament to describe the immaterial part of our being. Along with our physical being, we were designed to be "soulish" creatures. In the New Testament, this part of the nature of men is referred to by use of the Greek word *psyche*. Our English word *psychological* is derived from this Greek word. Human beings are psychological beings as well as physical beings. The immaterial part of our nature is every bit as important as the material part.

It is our soulish, or psychological, capacities that enable us to think and experience emotion. This part of our nature is often referred to in the Bible as the mind. Mind, when used in this sense, means far more than the physical brain. The mind of man enables him to be a rational and intellectual being like God himself. We think, we feel, and we act because God has created us to be living "beings."

The Spiritual Dimension

In recent years, the purely physical view of life has lost many advocates. A two-dimensional view of human nature has become more common. The origins of the personal dimensions of our nature are hotly debated, but at least the psychological part of our being is recognized as fundamental to who we are as human beings. Now we come to the real watershed of the Genesis passage.

In this brief passage, we are told that men are more than psychosomatic beings. The text reveals that God designed humanity to be three-dimensional. It was the breath of God, imparted to the physical creature, that made Adam a living soul. The breath of God spoken of in Genesis is a reference to the Spirit of God. The Hebrew words for "breath" and "spirit" are used interchangeably in the Old Testament. We were designed to be physical and emotional beings who have the capacity to possess God's Spirit. The presence of the Spirit made humans spiritual beings who possessed physical, psychological, and spiritual life.

If we are to live holistically, we must be operating as three-dimensional beings. We certainly need to be alive physically and emotionally, but we also need to be functioning spiritually. At the deepest level of our being we need to be connected with

God through the work of the Spirit. This three-dimensional nature could be diagrammed as follows:

Three-Dimensional Man

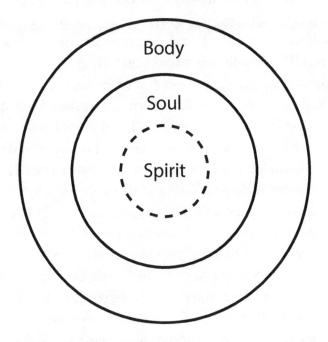

All three dimensions (physical, psychological, and spiritual) are critical. When the spiritual part of man is functioning properly, it is intended to influence the operation of the psychological, which in turn, dominates the physical. When all three are in sync, men are able to live holistically. The logical question becomes, "What went wrong?"

The Lost Dimension

Arthur Dent was right. Something is fundamentally wrong with the universe. In the Genesis account, we are told that God created man as a three-dimensional being, then placed him in

a Utopian environment, a beautiful garden called Eden. In this
Utopian environment, the Creator placed one restriction on the
man he had created. In the middle of this garden there was a tree
called the Tree of the Knowledge of Good and Evil. (I guarantee
you it was not an apple tree or symbol for sexual relations.)

God prohibited man from eating from this tree. He was very
clear that if his prohibition was violated, there would be horrible
consequences. Choosing to eat from the restricted tree would
constitute an act of moral disobedience, and such disobedience
carried with it a death sentence. "When you eat [from the tree]
you will surely die . . ." God said. (Gen. 2:17) Note that God did
not say, "I will kill you to punish you." He stated a fact. If Adam
and Eve chose to do what God told them not to—for their own
good—something radically catastrophic was going to happen.

In the third chapter of Genesis, we read the account of
what went wrong. Eve was tempted by the serpent to eat the
forbidden fruit. She convinced Adam to do the same. God had
told Adam if he ate he would die; the serpent told Eve that they
would not die. That was a lie. The serpent convinced Eve if she
and Adam ate the forbidden fruit, they would be like God. The
issue then was the same issue we face today: Who will be God
in our lives?

Adam chose to be his own god. The result was death.

If you read the text you might be thinking, "Wait a minute!
He didn't die." It is true that upon exercising his freedom
to disobey God, Adam did not die physically . . . yet. But
something radical took place within his inner being. Before,
he had enjoyed an intimate relationship with God; now he was
afraid of God. He even hid from God. When confronted, he
refused to get honest and instead made excuses for his behavior.
His fear of God and the rationalization of his behavior were

symptoms of the tragedy that had occurred in his inner being. Adam had died spiritually. Death is the absence of life. The Spirit is the source of spiritual life. The absence of the Spirit produces spiritual death. Adam became two-dimensional. As such, he was unable to enjoy the relationship with God he had enjoyed when he was whole.

The spiritual fragmentation of his inner life was reflected in the fact that he blamed Eve for the act of disobedience. Spiritual fragmentation leads to relational fragmentation. Blame and rationalization are usually recognized as signs of internal dysfunction. They are defense mechanisms used to protect damaged emotional systems.

What a dismal picture! In one act of willful disobedience, the first man created disharmony with God, with himself, with his spouse, and with his fellowman. You might say Adam broke ground for the construction of a street called the Boulevard of Broken Dreams.

Spiritual death radically alters the capacity of people to understand and live according to the blueprint God has designed. The very nature of humanity is distorted. When the core of personality is not under the dominant influence of the Spirit of God, the remaining dimensions experience distortion. Apart from God, people seek fulfillment in ways God never intended; ways that will never meet the deepest needs of the human heart.

Distortion within the spiritual dynamic produces distortion in the emotional system God created. The distortion of these dynamics seriously affects our lives. We get hooked into the Solomon Syndrome. As a result, we live in ways that are dissatisfying and unfulfilling.

But there is a way to get back to three-dimensional living. Albert Einstein once observed that the first step in discovering the solution to a problem is to identify the problem. If you are open to the possibility that the assumptions and observations presented in this chapter have some measure of validity, then you should be encouraged. Having identified the problem, we have the ability to make the adjustments necessary to move our lives back into the sphere of divine intervention and holistic living. Before we undertake that task, let's look at how the loss of the spiritual dimension has affected our psychological systems and the quality of our emotional lives.

Personal Reflection

I hope that what you have just read has created at least some sense of awareness concerning the spiritual dynamic of life. Now is a time to assess your own condition. Take time to read and reflect on the following questions. If you need to make an adjustment, you will find how to do so in the chapters that follow.

- Have you ever struggled with the meaning of life? Did you find an answer?
- Have you ever wondered about your own relationship with God?
- Are you currently living two-dimensionally or three-dimensionally?
- If God actually had a blueprint for your life, would you like to know what it is?

CHAPTER FOUR

We Are What We Think Other People Think We Are

(An Introduction to Self-Systems Thinking)

"How are you?" This is perhaps the most frequently asked question in the human social experience. "I'm fine. How are you?" This is probably the most frequent response to the most frequently asked question. It is also one of the most frequently told lies, equaled only by the response it asks for, which is usually "fine." In reality, most men and women are not fine. They are wounded, insecure, struggling, and don't feel very good about their lives or themselves.

Tim was a struggling pilgrim. For several years he had been attempting to be Christ's man. He faithfully read his

Bible. He worked at developing his prayer life. He did a pretty good job of living a life of willing obedience to God. The only thing he struggled with was the most important thing. Tim had a hard time loving people. His marriage was difficult. He felt defeated about the way he treated and sometimes mistreated his children. He had few close friends. Because he had been growing in his relationship with Christ, Tim recognized that his struggle to love was a serious problem. He also began to understand that he didn't love the one person who, along with Christ, he must love in order to authentically love anyone else: Tim didn't love himself.

"How are you feeling?" This was the question Tim was asked early every morning by the psychologist who guided a time of isolation and solitude. For twenty-one days, Tim lived in a small cabin in the mountains of Colorado. He lived in total isolation. There was no TV, no radio, no tape player, no books, phone, newspaper—not even a Bible. For twenty-one days he prayed, thought, reflected, and journaled. Tim was alone with himself and God. The experience was called an "intensive," and it is the only appropriate word to describe what those days were like for Tim and for other men and women who have used this spiritual exercise.

Tim learned many things about himself during those days. He learned how to honestly answer the question, "How are you feeling?" He learned the answer to that question has a great deal to do with the quality of his life. We all long to be able to honestly say, "I'm feeling good" when asked that question. Whether we are conscious of it or not, everyone wants to feel good. We want to feel good about life and we want to feel good about ourselves. Feelings play a central role in the quality of our lives. They are an integral part of our "self system." Our self system is composed of all the internal dynamics of our life that work together to give us a sense of who we are.

Altered States

"Who am I?"

"What am I doing here?"

"Why am I so confused?"

These are the questions that many men and women find themselves asking. When I first asked these questions in the early sixties I was not in a state of existential angst; I was actually regaining consciousness after being knocked out in a football game. Eventually, I would ask these questions in a more philosophical setting, but in 1964, I wasn't thinking very philosophically. I hadn't started the difficult struggle of defining my identity as a man. Identity, like emotion, is a central dynamic of the self-system.

"Who am I?"

"What am I doing here?"

"Why am I so confused?"

This time, it was the late sixties. I was a college student, sitting on the floor of a friend's house, listening to the Moody Blues. With my earphones on, and the volume cranked up, I was experiencing a significantly altered state of consciousness.

Within a matter of months, I would begin to discover the answers to those questions. This was the end of my pseudo-hippie phase, and I was trying to put life together in a way that made some sense. It wasn't working!

"Who am I?"

"What am I doing here?"

"Why am I so confused?"

The year was now 1975. I had been on my spiritual journey for nearly five years. I had been working fulltime in Christian ministry for three years. I had been married for a year-and-a-half. And yet, the answers to these questions were still not crystalized in my thinking. My wife, Allison, and I had taken a few months of sabbatical and moved to Washington, D.C., to live in an intentional community. We were pursuing a work-study program to attempt to get a firm fix on what the next phase of our lives should look like.

It was during these months that I set a personal goal of trying to understand what makes people "tick." I needed to know the answer to the questions I had been asking my own life, and I wanted to be able to help answer these questions for other men who seemed to be wrestling with the same issues.

During my quest, I began to understand what I now consider to be the most important dynamics of human motivation. I discovered that human behavior is motivated by certain needs, what I have previously called felt needs and what behavioral scientists have labeled real needs.

The pioneer of the need-motivated school of psychology was Abraham Maslow. In 1954, Maslow published his book, *Motivation and Personality*, in which he postulated his famous hierarchy of needs. Anyone who has ever endured a freshman psychology class has probably been exposed to Maslow's famous hierarchy. The hierarchy is usually diagrammed as a pyramid:

Maslow's Hierarchy of Needs

- Self-actualization
- Self-esteem
- Love & Belonging
- Security
- Physiological

The theory behind the hierarchy suggests that until our most basic needs are met, we are not able to move on to higher levels of growth and fulfillment. A starving man is not usually concerned with his sense of self-esteem. However, once the basic needs are met, a man or woman begins to pursue the higher needs. This drive toward what Maslow called self-actualization, and the needs that must be met to achieve actualization, form the underlying dynamics of the human motivational system according to Maslow's early work.

As illustrated in Maslow's schematic, once our basic physiological and safety needs have been met, the movement toward personal fulfillment passes through the twin needs of love and belongingness. Dr. Larry Crabb, in his book *Effective Biblical Counseling*, uses the terms "security" and "significance" to refer to these same dynamics. The need for security is a need for unconditional love. The need for significance is a need for meaning and purpose. Without a sense of security and a sense of significance, we cannot move on to a healthy sense of self-esteem. The longing for a positive sense of self-esteem is the underlying felt need that sets the cycle of human motivation into motion. I believe that Crabb, Maslow, and a host of others in the fields of psychology and psychiatry would agree.

In his later years, Maslow recognized that self-actualization was not the highest objective of human development and motivation. He began to talk in terms of self-transcendence, by which he meant that the ultimate objective of life was to live for something greater than ourselves. He was right on target.

You and I were not created simply to find our highest fulfillment in becoming self-actualized. If that is our goal, we will cheat ourselves out of the best life has to offer. Solomon was tremendously self-actualized. You and I were actually designed to be "God-actualized." We are not created to simply achieve human potential; we are created to achieve our God-designed potential.

One of the loftiest statements in the history of human literature is the statement "in the image of God he created him; male and female he created them." (Gen. 1:27) Humanity was made in the image of God. The theological concept of the image of God has a multitude of implications.

That men and women exist as personal beings is a reflection of the fact that we are made in the image of God. Human personality, with its intellect, emotions, and power of will, reflects the nature and image of God. The moral dimension of human existence with its sense of "oughtness" (i.e., right and wrong) is an expression of the moral nature of God. You and I were intended to be a reflection of the glory and nature of God. This does not mean, as some have mistakenly assumed, that we are God. Someone once humorously observed that there are two fundamental principles of human enlightenment: #1—*There is a God*; and #2—*You are not Him!* We are not God, but in many ways we are like God, because God designed us to exist in his image.

A number of years ago, I had the privilege of getting to know Robert Schuller, pastor of the "Crystal Cathedral." Dr. Schuller taught the human drive for self-actualization is simply the reflection of the image of God in man. He called it "the hunger for glory." When we piece together the psychological insights concerning self-esteem with the theology of the image of God we begin to see that our self-concept and how we feel about ourselves is actually a spiritual issue. Self-esteem is "felt" at an emotional level, but it is rooted in a much deeper dimension of our being. Because of the centrality of these issues, it is important to understand how our self-concept is developed.

The Dynamics of Self-Concept

Humanity is endowed with a unique ability that is both a blessing and a curse. Our intellectual abilities make us capable of being self-conscious. Technically that means that we have the ability to examine our own self and form opinions and feelings about who we are. Those opinions and feelings lie at the heart of the human quest for personal fulfillment.

Self-Image

The human mind goes through a logical process to arrive at the internal mental image we call the "self." The first step in the process involves the construction of an internal mental image of who we are. This internal picture is often called our self-image. Self-image is a highly complex internalized perception. Note the word *perception*; self-image is perceptually based. It may or may not have any objective basis, but is almost entirely subjective.

Christine has lived on a treadmill of repeated failure for many years. One look in her eyes (if you can get her to look you in the eyes) tells you that she is not a happy camper. Everything about your first encounter with Christine would lead you to label her a "loser." What you can't see by looking at her is how she came to be the way she is.

Christine believes she *is* a loser. It is a primary component of her self-image. It was a message she heard from her earliest childhood. Abandoned at birth, Christine spent her early years in a string of abusive foster homes. The abuse was never blatant; social services made sure physical abuse was not tolerated. Emotional abuse is more difficult to detect. In Christine's case, it was primarily a function of neglect.

She was born with special needs. Had she been raised in the proper environment, her learning disabilities might have been detected early. If she had parents who cared, special help could have been found to help her learn to succeed in school. Her life, in all probability, would have turned out quite different. Instead, Christine failed. Her teachers and foster parents formed the opinion that she was stupid. This opinion was communicated consistently to Christine by every look they gave and every word they spoke. She came to believe that she was stupid and that she would always be a loser. This conviction lies at the heart of Christine's self-image. Her life has been one long, self-fulfilling prophecy flowing from this perception.

Ironically and tragically, Christine is actually quite intelligent. When her intelligence was finally tested, she scored in the superior range. Unfortunately, Christine was convinced the tests were wrong. Her perception was stronger than the hard data.

Internally, it is our perception that is real to us. For instance, one of the more common eating disorders our culture has spawned is called *anorexia nervosa*. One component of this very complicated disorder is the perception that one is obese. Most people who suffer from this disorder eventually have the appearance of a concentration camp survivor. Yet when they look in the mirror, they see a "fat" person. Perception forms their "reality," even though their perception has no basis in objective fact. It is critical to understand that self-concept is much like this eating disorder. It is an internal perception that does not necessarily have a basis in objective reality.

Another critical dimension of self-concept we see demonstrated in Christine's case is the fact that perception is developed primarily through reflected appraisal. Our self-concept is the product of what we think others think about us.

Again, our appraisal might be horribly skewed. Dr. Vernon Grounds, former President and Chancellor of Denver Seminary, has observed, "We are not who we think we are; and we are not who others think we are. We are who we think others think we are." The self-image is an internal picture of what we perceive to be our strengths, weaknesses, adequacies, attractiveness, intelligence, goodness, value, and lovability. Our mind, in all its warped and wonderful complexity, puts all this perceived data together and forms this internal image we call the self.

Self-Worth

Self-image breaks down into further subcategories based on what our mind does with this internal perceived image. Having formed an internal picture of who we are, our mind also forms an image of who we think we should be. Somewhere in our inner being is a reservoir of all the "shoulds," "oughts," "dos," "don'ts," "goods," and "bads" of a lifetime. Freud called this component of the psyche the superego. One psychologist refers to this factor of our internal landscape as "Super You." Again, as a product of perception and reflected appraisal, you and I have this internalized image of who we think we should be. Here comes the kicker! Along with the capability the brain possesses to form these two internal images, it has the ability to compare the two and evaluate the inevitable discrepancy between the perceived self (who we think we are) and the ideal self (who we think we should be).

Once we begin to compare our image of who we think we are with our image of who we think we should be, we begin to place a sense of value on our self. This attachment of value to our self-image produces our sense of self-worth.

Dan feels worthless. Not many people know how Dan feels; he covers it well with bravado. This feeling of worthlessness has been a constant source of relational difficulties in Dan's life.

The reasons Dan feels worthless are complex. To simplify, Dan has an unrealistic internal image of who he should be. This image is a product, primarily, of neurotic parenting within a dysfunctional family. Unrealistic goals and expectations were "programmed" into Dan at a very early age. His mental "tape recorder" is filled with "should" and "oughts" and "why didn't yous." When Dan compares his perceived self with his ideal self, he always falls short. Dan needs some help unraveling this problem.

Self-worth is that part of the self-concept that bridges the gap between the cognitive (or thinking) area and the affective (or feeling) dimension of self-concept. Our sense of self-worth places a heartfelt evaluation on who we are. Our evaluation will either be positive, generating a sense of value and worth, or, like Christine and Dan, the evaluation will be negative, creating a sense of personal unworthiness or worthlessness. For most of us, this evaluation is something of a mixed bag. Isn't the mind a wonderful thing?

Self-Esteem

One final process in the mind's formation of the self-concept remains to be mentioned. First, having formed a perceived internal image of who we think we are and who we think we should be, then having evaluated the discrepancy between the two and having attached a perceived value to our person, some bizarre part of the brain then attaches a feeling component to the whole package. If life (and our mom and dad) has been kind, we might be among the lucky carbon-based life forms on the planet who actually feel good enough about themselves to move toward living out their full God-given potential.

If, on the other hand, the experiences of life have been less than kind, and if we have had the bad fortune of growing up in a less than functional or a non-nurturing home, chances are that our self-esteem will be low and our emotional life will be something of a struggle. We will not feel good about ourselves. Since this factor is so powerful, many men and women go through life engaging in some of the most bizarre enterprises imaginable in order to feel good about themselves. This is not how the system was designed.

This component of our inner world is perhaps the single most significant motivating dynamic of life. The need for a positive sense of self-esteem will unconsciously drive much of our behavior. How we seek to get this need met will depend on the second factor in the cycle of human motivation. All of us carry around certain basic assumptions about life inside our heads and hearts. These assumptions constitute our belief system. This belief system dictates how we seek to meet the need for self-esteem. Remember Norma Jean?

There are only two options concerning the source of our personal belief systems. One is humanistic; the other is spiritually based. Most of us spend a great many years pursuing the humanistic options. When they fail to meet the deepest needs of our lives, we hopefully begin to seek something that transcends humanistic theories.

This pursuit will eventually lead us to seek spiritual answers to the questions we ask. We begin to question whether or not there might not be a divine design for living. We might even begin to wonder if God has designed a way to live that will fully meet these deep needs. Many men and women have discovered there is an affirmative answer to these questions. This discovery often reveals that our basic assumptions about how to get our needs met are not consistent with the "blueprint" we discover. At that point, we will have a very important decision to make. Are we going to live our lives on the basis of faulty assumptions, or are we willing to live consistently with what God has designed to meet our needs and move us toward full actualization and on to transcendence? The answer to that question will shape the course of our lives. Coming to terms with these issues requires some time of reflection and assessment.

At the heart of how we feel about ourselves is our experience of love. However, I would suggest that our need for love exceeds the human capability to give love. If we are going to feel good about ourselves, we will need to tap into a source of overpowering love. Such a source exists. This realization takes place as we take the time to stop and assess, "How am I really feeling?" and as we ask the tough question, "Is the course of my life leading me into the sources that will meet my real needs?" Such a course exists. It is found in prioritizing a network of relationships God designed to meet our deepest needs. How we interact with this network will make all the difference in the quality of our existence and how we feel about life and ourselves.

Personal Reflection

Before moving on, take a few minutes to reflect on what you've read in this chapter. Here are a few questions you might ask yourself:

- Do you have a conscious understanding of your needs?
- At what level on Maslow's hierarchy do you see yourself?

- How do you feel about yourself?
- Do you consider yourself a valuable person?
- Is your belief system working to meet your deepest needs?

CHAPTER FIVE

Buckets, Ladders, and Paradigm Shifts

(Understanding the Relational Network)

A t age thirty-seven, Jim came to realize that a spiritual solution existed that addressed life's challenges. Through a group of friends, he came to understand what it meant to have a personal relationship with Jesus Christ. Jim gave his life to Christ and began growing spiritually. As his relationship with Christ matured, Jim found himself forced to make a decision that would forever alter the course of his life. He had to decide whether he would seek to discover and live a life based on God's design or whether he would continue to live according to the chaotic plan he had been following for years.

Jim was wrestling with his belief system. Thinking through this decision, Jim had the good fortune of having one of those rare moments of clarity that seem to come all too infrequently in life. He thought, "If this is true, what could be more important than discovering God's plan?" Not too profound, but for Jim it was just that simple.

For the next few years, Jim studied great amounts of data relating to the whole subject of God's plan. For the first time ever, he began to read the Bible. He had picked the book up once or twice before but never seemed able to make any sense out of it. He always seemed to turn to some long and obscure genealogy, which seemed completely irrelevant to the real issues of life. Now, with a new commitment to discovering a spiritually based plan for his life, the book came alive.

Jim also devoured a great number of books on a wide variety of subjects relating to spiritual issues. It seemed the more he read and studied, the more there was for him to understand. Jim began to feel that perhaps God's plan was so complex that it would take a lifetime to figure out. At about the same time in his spiritual journey, Jim was exposed to a relatively simple framework that tied together the vast amount of data his brain had accumulated. At a men's Bible study, he heard his pastor teach on the subject of relational priorities. The message was based on an incident that occurred in the life of Christ.

One day, Jesus was asked what is surely the best question anyone ever asked a man who claimed to be the Son of God. Matthew relates that an expert in the Law tested Jesus with this inquiry: "Teacher, which is the greatest commandment in the Law?" (Matt. 22:36) As Jim listened to his pastor, he found himself wondering if the motivation for asking this question might have been born of the same frustration he was experiencing. After all, think about all the data this "expert" had accumulated over the years. Dr. Bob told the men to think of the question paraphrased like this: "If you take all the information in this big book and boil it down to its essence, is there any unifying principle that ties it all together?" This was the question Jim had been asking himself for several years.

Jesus told the scribe (the meaning of the NIV phrase translated "expert in the law") the first and greatest commandment is to, "Love the Lord your God with all your heart and with all your soul and with all your mind." (Matt. 22:37–38) He continued by adding that there was a second command of like significance: "Love your neighbor as yourself." (Matt. 22:39) Bob told the men that the purpose of life, according to Jesus, is to love God and to love each other. Loving relationships are at the heart of the divine design for life. Suddenly, Jim knew what he had been looking for was amazingly simple. He needed to learn what it meant to love God and his neighbor.

Back to the Garden

If we examine the creation account of Genesis and look at it through the filter of Jesus' statements, we can see how God developed a perfect system in which all of our needs for love and meaning were intended to be met in an amazing network of relationships.

We have already seen how the second chapter of Genesis gives us a picture and explanation of who we were intended to be. We were designed by God to be three-dimensional beings: body, soul, and spirit. We have also made note of the mind-boggling truth that as three-dimensional beings we were created in the very image or reflection of our Creator. Now, as we read on in this second chapter of Genesis we will discover a strategy for how we were intended to live.

Having created the man, God designed and developed a Utopian environment in which he placed Adam. Living in relationship with the living God and experiencing what seems to be very clear communication with him, Adam was also assigned the task of working in this environment to take care of it. When we reach the eighteenth verse of this chapter we read what is perhaps one of the most significant statements in all the Bible.

Up until this point, every act of God and every product of His creative exercise had been evaluated by God as "good." Five times in the first chapter of Genesis we read the phrase, ". . . and God saw that it was good." Finally, after the creation of man, God appraised all that he had made and said, "It was *very* good." (Gen. 1:31, italics mine)

When we get to the eighteenth verse of the second chapter, we read for the first time that something about creation was found to be problematic. God said, "It is *not good* for the man to be alone." In response to this evaluation, God put Adam to sleep and created Eve; interpersonal relationships were born. God then personally presided over the first wedding, and the covenant of marriage was established. With marriage came the possibility for the creation of families. As families grew, an intermarried community could develop. In these short verses, we see the raw material for living according to a set of divinely ordained priorities. Let's put it together.

First, God provided a primary and secondary channel for meeting man's need for love. The primary channel for meeting this need was to be a man's personal relationship with God. We were created to live in loving relationship with God. The critical word here is relationship. God is not primarily interested in what we believe or don't believe. God is not primarily interested in what we do or don't do. God is primarily interested in us. He created us to live in a love relationship with Him. What God desires is to love us and have us receive and respond to his love with our love. This is why Jesus had to remind the experts that the heart of the issue was to "love God with all your heart." The central message of the Bible is "Love God, and let God love you!"

Many men and women have a difficult time making the mental transition from viewing God as a demanding tyrant or celestial policeman to understanding that he is a loving Father. This transition is the pivotal internal change that will begin to move us toward a life that is consistent with the spiritual blueprint. Without an experience of the unconditional love of God, we will never fully have our need for love or security met. Regardless of how rich our interpersonal relationships are, they are never perfectly unconditional. Only God can love us unconditionally. The ultimate expression of God's unconditional love was the gift of his Son, Jesus. In the life and death of Jesus, we are able to see and experience perfect unconditional love. Through a relationship with Jesus Christ, we are able to experience spiritual life and fellowship with God. This relationship becomes the foundation for living according to the divine blueprint. It also forms the first rung on a conceptual ladder that will help you understand how the network of relationships God has established fits together.

The Hierarchy of Love

The network of relationships God designed to meet our needs contains a sequence of priorities. Jesus clearly told the scribe that the first and greatest commandment was to love God with our whole being. (Matt. 22:37) He then went on to say a second command was like it: "Love your neighbor as yourself." (Matt. 22:38) The word "neighbor" encompasses all human relationships.

Within this broad category is a biblical sequence of priority. If you are married, your husband or wife is your "neighbor." If you have children, your sons and daughters are your "neighbors." If you are part of a church, your spiritual brothers and sisters are your "neighbors." Your real-life neighbors are also your "neighbors," and the person who works at the filling station where you buy gas is your "neighbor." As a matter of fact, even people on the other side of the planet, living in cultures radically different from your own, are your "neighbors."

Each of these categories of "neighbor" fits within a system of priorities mapped out for us in the Bible. Visually and conceptually, this system of priorities can be illustrated by using the image of a ladder. My partner in ministry, Bo Mitchell, coined the term "The Ladder of Love."

Ladder of Love
The Relationship Paradigm

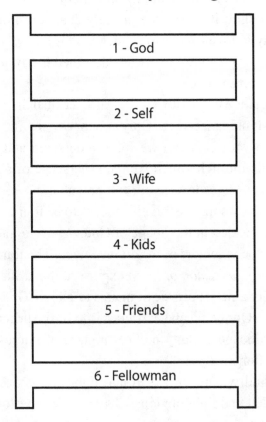

1 - God

2 - Self

3 - Wife

4 - Kids

5 - Friends

6 - Fellowman

Each rung on the ladder represents a category of relationships set in its proper place of priority. This tool can serve as a mental filter through which we view the world and with which we are able to prioritize how we are going to live our lives.

Priority #1

The top rung of the ladder represents the highest priority relationship of life. Above and beyond all the factors that contribute to living consistently in the will of God, our direct, immediate, and personal relationship with God is to hold the preeminent place. This relationship is not only the top priority in the paradigm; it is also the primary channel through which our security or love need is to be met. God is ready, willing, and able to love us unconditionally. He designed the system, and he is able to meet the need.

This relationship with God is also critical in getting our need for significance met. Only when we are in the proper relationship with God can we fully understand and enter into the channels through which we gain the sense of significance that moves our lives toward our full potential.

Our primary source of significance is to be found in the truth that we are created in the image of God. We were intended and designed to be reflectors of the divine image. The framers of the *Westminster Confession of Faith* expressed this truth by stating that the chief aim or purpose of man is to glorify God and enjoy him forever. Our being and existence is to be the primary source of our significance. Many biblical images of purpose support this conviction.

Jesus said we are to be salt and light in the world. (Matt. 5:13–14) Salt and light obviously have tasks to perform, which fall into the category of "doing," but it is the very nature of salt and light that enable them to perform these tasks. Therefore, "if the salt loses its saltiness," it is no longer good for accomplishing its task. Salt must be salt!

In the New Testament, the apostle Paul writes about the experience of Moses when he received the law of God. Having been in the presence of God, Moses came down the mountain reflecting and radiating the glory of God. Paul draws the conclusion that the purpose of our existence is to reflect the Lord's glory, like Moses, as we are transformed into his image.

(2 Cor. 3:18) By our very being, we are to reflect the glory of God. Obviously, something has gone wrong. But remember, we are exploring the original intentions of God and the systems he designed to enable people to live meaningfully and significantly.

Every human being is of eternal significance to God because every human being, however flawed and imperfect, bears something of the divine image. Every man or woman living on the planet, simply by virtue of his or her existence, is significant. As one small child observed, "God made me and he doesn't make any junk!" Only in the proper relationship with God do these realities begin to come into focus and affect our experience. Ultimately, our self systems are dependent upon spiritual realities.

Along with these lofty callings to be image bearers and to live in relationship with God, secondary channels for meeting both the need for security and the need for significance were put in place in this relational network.

Priority #2

When Jesus stated that the purpose of life was to love God and one another, he added a qualifying statement. Jesus said we should love our neighbor as ourselves. (Matt. 22:39) The question has been repeatedly raised in both theological and psychological circles whether it is even possible to love one's neighbor without a healthy sense of self-love. Previously I attempted to develop a brief overview of the dynamics of the self system. Let me add one further dimension to the matrix of self-image, self-worth, and self-esteem. Self-love is the fourth logical component of the self system.

When exploring the concept of self-love, a fundamental decision must be made. With what content do you load the word "love?" If love is given a cultural definition, self-love becomes self-centered and narcissistic. Self-love defined egocentrically becomes unhealthy and destructive. Since the entire biblical frame of reference negates self-centeredness, loving one's self must be defined differently. When love is given its proper definition, self-love is perfectly consistent with God's plans and purpose.

When Jesus spoke to the scribe about loving, he used the Greek word *agape*. This kind of love seeks the highest welfare of the object loved. It is an action-oriented word that requires an act of the will. If the object loved is yourself, then to love yourself means to seek your own highest welfare. Since the will of God for our lives is the best life possible, if we truly love ourselves with *agape* love, we will seek God's will. This is the definition of self-love that permeates the divine blueprint. God's will for our lives calls us to deny ourselves. We are instructed to say "no" to self-will and "yes" to God's will. In doing so we learn to die to self. At first glance it might look like a contradiction in terms when the Bible tells us to both love ourselves and deny ourselves. Actually, these two commands perfectly complement one another.

In one of the most complex statements Jesus made, he told his followers that whoever tried to save his life would lose it, but whoever lost his life for Jesus' sake would find it. (Luke 9:24) The irony of the self relationship is that it is the one relationship in the relational paradigm whose needs can never be met by concentrating directly on them. The needs of the self are actually met in the process of dying to self and investing in and concentrating on the other priority relationships of the paradigm.

I often think of this paradox by using the image of a series of buckets that need to be filled. The more we try to fill the self bucket, the emptier it gets. Finally, when we give up on filling the self bucket and begin to concentrate on the other buckets (God, marriage, family, friends, and fellow human), guess what happens? While filling the other buckets, the self bucket has been mysteriously filled; it is in losing our life (self) that we find our life (self). This is the beauty and irony of the self relationship. To love yourself (that is, seek God's best for yourself), concentrate on the other priorities of the pyramid.

Priority #3

When God made the statement, "it is not good for man to be alone," he had already entered into a relationship with Adam. The primary channel for meeting humanity's need for love was in place. God then designed a series of human relationships to serve as the secondary channels for meeting that need. The man was put to sleep and a part of his being was removed and fashioned into a woman. From one came two, who were brought back together to become one. The marriage relationship was designed and instituted. For those of us who are married, this relationship is intended to be our highest priority after our relationship with Christ.

If you are single, you face two exciting possibilities. It is possible that some day you will be married. At that point, your marriage will become a major priority. On the other hand, God's plan for your life might be for you to stay single. In that case God, himself, will occupy this space in a special way. It is clear in the Bible that Jesus was single. The Father's plans for his earthly life required that Jesus not have a physical wife and family.

The apostle Paul was most likely also single. It is possible that at one time, he was married, but by the time he wrote his letters, he was single. God's plan for his life also necessitated that he remained single. I think it would be safe to say that both Jesus and Paul, along with many men and women throughout the ages, have lived full and meaningful lives without being married. Biblically, both marriage and singleness are viewed as special callings from God.

For those of us who have the calling to married life, our spouse is to be our highest earthly priority; for those who are called to be single, relationships with friends and fellowman assume a higher priority.

Priority #4

The next rung on the ladder represents our relationships with our children. For those of us who are parents, our children are to be our highest priority after our spouse. When God designed the marriage relationship, he designed humans with the capacity to "be fruitful and increase in number." (Gen. 1:28) God created families as a secondary channel to meet our needs for love and significance. The family was intended to form the nucleus of God's design for the human community. Our children are a vital part of God's system of priorities. Learning to make our children the priority God intended them to be is not only important, it is one of the great sources of joy and fulfillment in life.

Priority #5

As families grew and multiplied, human community was created. I believe God intended the world to be filled with communities of people that love and serve him and one another. These communities provide increased opportunities for relationships. In the midst of the community, we need a few close friendships to help us be the men and women God intended us to be. We need each other. In our fast-paced, technological world, community does not come naturally. If we are to experience what the Bible calls fellowship, it will take determination on our part. Making our relationships with a small number of other men or women (I recommend same-sex relationships in this context) a priority is a major component of the blueprint and another important factor in getting our needs for love and meaning met.

Priority #6

The final rung of the ladder is entitled "Fellowman." This is an extremely comprehensive term. It is also a critically important term. By acknowledging this rung on the ladder, we are making a statement about the value of all people and the priority of relationships over productivity or accumulation.

In our culture, we are constantly bombarded with the false message that living well hinges on the accumulation of "stuff." Many people go through life with the often unconscious philosophy of "love things, use people." The fellowman rung will require a change in our thinking. It requires a commitment to a new philosophy of "love people, use things," finding significance through the secondary channel of serving people.

These six areas of relationship (God, self, marriage, family, friends, and fellowman) form a relational network. They constitute a framework of priorities designed by God to make life full and meaningful. The choice to make these relationships the priorities of our lives constitutes a radical paradigm shift. Our convictions about these issues inform and redefine our belief system. The goals we set and the actions we take to meet these goals transform our lifestyles. Life viewed through this filter and lived according to these priorities looks radically different from life lived in conformity to the mold of culture.

Every decision you make has implications for some relationship on the ladder. If you have a major decision to make, you can evaluate the decision on the basis of how this decision will affect your relationship with God. Will the change enhance or detract from your ability to love and serve God? Is the change motivated by an egocentric desire to inflate your own sense of self-esteem and meet your own ego needs? Does the change have any negative impact on the time and energy you will have available to cultivate your relationships with your wife and children?

The ladder is of equal value in making a decision as simple as responding to an invitation to go fishing on Saturday. If the invitation comes from a friend whose relationship is a priority on the ladder you will have a strong tendency to make an affirmative decision. But before you say "yes," you need to decide whether spending the day with your wife and children is what you really need to be doing. The beauty of having a tool like this lies in the fact that if you have already been concentrating on these priorities daily, your relationship with your family might already have received adequate time and energy. You will then be free to enjoy that occasional Saturday on the river or golf course without guilt or remorse.

This ladder of relational priorities is a tool you can use to assess where your life is heading. If the actual priorities of your life are out of alignment with this relational filter, then you know it is time for some adjustment. As we move on through this book I will make some suggestions about how to accomplish that task.

To the extent that your life is built on a commitment to making these relationships the priorities of your life, you will be well on the way to living a life of substance and significance. You will be building a better life for yourself, your wife or husband, your children, your friends, your community, and the world. To the extent you are structuring your life on a set of priorities shaped by some other factor, you will probably find that you are heading down a Boulevard of Broken Dreams, well on the way to a life of disillusionment, frustration, and even despair. In the second part of this book I am going to walk you through each relationship in the network. Before I do, however, it would be helpful to look at a few steps that need to be taken at this point to break out of the Solomon Syndrome and make the following chapters most helpful.

Personal Reflection

If the ideas presented in this chapter are new to you, it might be helpful to spend a few minutes reflecting before moving on. Here are a few questions related to this chapter to use in your time of assessment:

- Do you understand the concept of a relationship with God?
- Who are the people God has placed in your relational paradigm?
- What are the top priorities of your life as reflected by your use of time, money, and energy?
- Is there anything in the way you are living that you would like to change?

CHAPTER SIX

Exit This Way

(Four Steps to Make the Break)

Nearly twenty years ago, Bill was running down the Boulevard of Broken Dreams at full speed. He had spent years building a successful business as a manufacturer's representative for a computer company. He had also spent years neglecting his wife and children while developing a tidy package of very bad habits. He drank too much, smoked too much, dabbled in drug use, and chased other women. One night, Bill had an experience for which he will be eternally grateful. Bill pulled over, out of the fast lane, and paused long enough to take a look at where he was heading. What he observed was so distressing that it changed the course of his life.

Bill saw that the world was in trouble! He thought about what life must have been like before there were cars, trucks, roads, and buildings. He thought about the raw material of life on the planet and the potential that once existed for the development of a civilized world. Then Bill compared the potential with what actually existed.

He seemed to see life through a different set of lenses that night. He was beginning to experience a paradigm shift. Everything looked warped and distorted. He watched rusted and dented cars roll down cracked and potholed streets. The cars appeared to be occupied by unhappy and distraught people who seemed to be in a great hurry to get nowhere.

Bill looked at the landscape and saw chaotically designed houses and buildings in a state of disrepair and disintegration. There was no evidence of the beauty of nature. Like the cars, the buildings appeared to be filled with men and women who spent much of their days doing unfulfilling work in order to buy things they didn't need and that would never make them happy. It was a very bleak set of images.

But the bleakness of that picture was nothing compared to what Bill saw when he looked within. He saw himself in those cars, houses, and office buildings. He began to realize that he had no idea what life was about. At first, this was a horribly depressing experience; he realized he was heading nowhere fast. In a state of near despair, he realized he didn't know how to change his course or whether there was a way of life that made sense. It was what I have come to identify as a rare moment of clarity.

Fortunately, Bill made two critical decisions that night. First, he put the brakes on his life. He simply stopped running down the road. He was no longer willing to accept the status quo and pursue a meaningless life simply because it was the norm. Second, Bill made a decision to attempt to discover if life had meaning and purpose. He wanted to know if there was a way of life that was meaningful and significant. Without much of a spiritual background, he decided he needed to know if there was a God and if so, what he was like.

Over time, Bill discovered life doesn't need to be chaotic and meaningless. He found an approach to living that has been proven solid and substantive to him for over twenty years.

The preceding chapters of this book contain much of what Bill began to discover that night. Bill is one of the lucky few who came to realize he needed to make a break from the Solomon Syndrome. Let me walk you through the decisions Bill made to make that break.

DECISION ONE: Becoming Three-Dimensional

To break away from the Solomon Syndrome and begin to develop a life structure consistent with the divine blueprint, we must first make sure we are three-dimensional men and women. We have seen that the intention of God is for us to be spiritual beings. But by nature we are not.

In what at first seems like a contradiction, the Bible tells us every man and woman on the planet is born dead. We are alive physically but dead spiritually. Understanding this fact will help us understand why Jesus told a man named Nicodemus that the missing ingredient in his quest for the kingdom of God was a second birth experience. (John 3:3) Nicodemus had been born physically, but he had never experienced spiritual birth. What was true of Nicodemus is also true of you and me.

One of the clearer images explaining how to become three-dimensional again is found in the New Testament book of

Revelation. In the third chapter of this book, Jesus Christ paints a word picture of what needs to happen in each of our lives if we are to become spiritual people. Jesus says, "Here I am! I stand at the door and knock." (Rev. 3:20) The door Jesus is referring to is a symbolic door; you might imagine it as the door to your heart or inner being. Jesus is knocking on this door because he wants to enter our lives and give us spiritual life. He goes on to tell us what must happen in order for us to experience spiritual birth: "If anyone hears my voice and opens the door, I will come in." (Rev. 3:20)

We must respond to Christ by making a decision to personally invite him to invade our lives. When we do, he will enable our innermost being to come alive spiritually by means of the person of the Holy Spirit. When the Spirit comes, he imparts spiritual life to us. His very presence in our inner being makes us three-dimensional once again.

Three-Dimensional Man

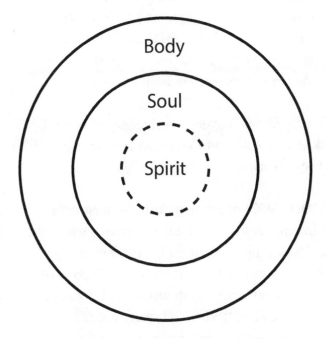

When Bill reached the point in his life where he knew something needed to change, he decided to visit a church attended by several of his coworkers. One of these men had very tactfully and sensitively communicated to Bill that he would always be welcome there. When the time came, Bill knew where to go.

That morning the minister explained how to make this decision. Bill sensed God had orchestrated the message just for him. At the end of the message, the minister invited anyone who had never asked Christ into his or her life to pray this prayer with him:

> *Lord Jesus, I need you. Thank you for dying*
> *on the cross for me. I want to turn from my self-*
> *centered and self-directed life and follow you.*
> *Come into my life, Lord Jesus. I open the door*
> *and receive you as Savior and Lord. I want to be*
> *the kind of person you want me to be.*

Bill prayed this prayer with sincerity of heart. By doing so, he took the first step in the adjustment process. His life has never been the same.

DECISION TWO: Affirming Your Real Needs

By inviting Jesus Christ into our lives we take the first step toward developing a relationship with the living God. We are then enabled to begin to see life from God's point of view as we come alive spiritually. This in turn will help each of us answer the critical question, "What do I really need?"

Bill didn't realize that by receiving the new life Christ gives, he actually met the greatest real need in his life. As he began to grow spiritually, his understanding of his other needs also fell into place. Bill came to understand that all men, himself included, have the twin needs of unconditional love and meaning. By identifying and embracing these two needs as the most important needs of his emotional life, Bill made the second decision in the process of life structuring. Only as we identify and affirm our real needs are we able to develop a belief system that is in harmony with the relational paradigm. If we plug these two factors into a schematic of human motivation it looks like this:

Dynamics of Human Motivation

```
  ┌─────────────┐
  │   Needs     │──── Produce ───▶  ┌──────────────┐
┌──────┐ ┌──────────┐              │ Belief System │
│ Love │─│ Meaning  │              └──────────────┘
└──────┘ └──────────┘                     │
Boulevard   Meets                     Generates
of Broken                                 │
 Dreams ◀                                 ▼
  ┌─────────────┐              ┌──────────────┐
  │  Behavior   │◀── Lead to ──│    Goals     │
  └─────────────┘              └──────────────┘
```

Decision One changes our entire perspective of the nature of life. Decision Two clearly identifies the first components of the human motivation system. We are now ready to move to the critical third decision in the adjustment process.

DECISION THREE: Redefining Your Belief System

Bill began to make choices about how he was going to get his real needs met. He wanted to develop a belief system that was filled with a commitment to God's plan for his life. He wanted to replace his "bad theology and geometry" with the truth. Bill began making the third decision.

How are you going to live? How are you going to invest your time, energy, and resources? At this point, you will want to plug the relational network of the ladder of love into your personal philosophy of life. This decision further refines our motivational schematic to look like this:

Dynamics of Human Motivation

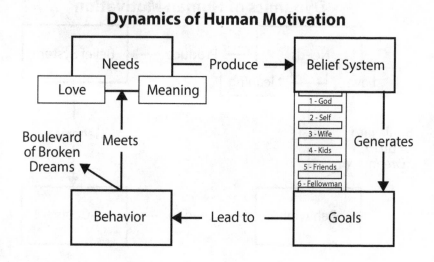

In a biblically based life structure, our relationship with God is to be our highest priority. We need to take the time, exert the energy, and invest the resources necessary to develop our spiritual lives. We must determine that we will heavily invest our primary resources in this divinely ordained network of relationships. When this network becomes intimately integrated into our belief system, we are ready to make the fourth decision.

DECISION FOUR: Building Priority Relationships

The fourth decision requires action. Bill's new belief system led him to make some choices and institute some new behaviors that reflected his new philosophy of life. If we have adopted the conceptual elements of the divine blueprint, Decision Four will require actions that develop this network of relationships.

Two key words permeated Bill's process of setting new goals that were consistent with his new priorities. The first word was *love*. Bill recognized that it was his job to implement behaviors that would build loving relationships on every rung of the ladder. Love is an action word. Bill recognized that he needed to invest time and energy in these relationships to genuinely know and authentically care for the people God had placed in his life.

The second key word for Bill was *serve*. Love always leads to engagement. Bill began to shift the focus in his relationships in order to reach out and care for the people in his network. He began to discover that his commitment to serve affected his own need for personal significance. Bill began to feel his life was really counting for something important.

What would all of this look like for you? It probably will look a little different for each of us. In the second part of this book, I am going to take each rung of the ladder and help you see what making these relationships a priority might look like. I also hope to give you some ideas on how to cultivate these relationships in your own life.

If you make these four decisions—(1) become a three-dimensional person, (2) identify and affirm your real needs, (3) develop a spiritually-based belief system, and (4) begin to build priority relationships—I can promise you this: You will be able to break out of the Solomon Syndrome. In a very real sense, you will take the exit off the Boulevard of Broken Dreams marked "A Better Life." You will head down a road that will lead to a life of meaning, satisfaction, and personal fulfillment. You will start to live in a way that reaps the benefits of living according to God's divine blueprint.

Personal Reflection

You are now at a critical juncture in this book. In the next chapters you will have the opportunity to look at each major area of relationship in your life. Before you move on, use this time to honestly assess your life. Reflect on the following questions:

- Are you ready to make significant changes in your life?
- Have your made a decision like Bill did regarding his relationship with God?
- If not, would you like to ask Christ into your life? Here is the prayer Bill prayed. You can pray it now:

    Lord Jesus, I need you. Thank you for dying on the cross for me. I want to turn from my self-centered and self-directed life and follow you. Come into my life, Lord Jesus. I open the door and receive you as Savior and Lord. I want to be the kind of man or woman you want me to be. I want to live according to your divine blueprint.

- Carefully look at each of the four decisions in this chapter. Have you made each one?

PART TWO

Bridges, Networks, and Promises Kept

———————

A Tool for Adjustment

CHAPTER SEVEN

Making Love Last

(What Solomon Never Knew)

The scenario is repeated on numerous occasions. A boy and girl meet, fall in love, and make that monumental decision to get married. The date is set, arrangements are made, tuxedos are rented, and invitations are sent. Finally, the big day arrives. In the presence of friends and family, the boy and girl look into each other's eyes and say those magic words, "I do." The guests throw rice, set butterflies free, or blow bubbles, the couple jumps in the getaway car, and they live happily ever after. Wouldn't it be great if that was the way it always worked?

Unfortunately, all too often the smiling faces of the wedding day turn into the disappointed and angry faces of the attorney's office. It should not be that way. In his somewhat offbeat love story, *Still Life with the Woodpecker*, Tom Robbins observes that the great question in the last quarter of the twentieth century is "How do you make love last?" This is an immensely significant observation. What was true in the last quarter of the twentieth century remains true in the first quarter of the twenty-first.

Every day I hear of another marriage that has ended in divorce. As I drive by a nearby elementary school, I see children on their way home to spend the rest of the evening without either a mom or a dad. In one nearby high school, eighty percent of the students live in single-parent homes. Why do so many marriages fail? I believe it is because we have not learned how to answer the question: "How do you make love last?"

I know the pain of this struggle. There was a time in my own marriage when I wondered whether or not my wife and I were going to make it. By the grace of God, and with the help of a few good friends (some of whom we paid at the rate of a hundred and fifty dollars an hour!), we worked hard to find the answer to that question. Our commitment to the principles contained in the first part of this book made the difference between becoming another divorce statistic or molding our marriage into a healthy and vital relationship. Let me share with you what I've learned about how to make love last.

The Great American Myth

The problems that lead to the loss of love begin with the tremendous misunderstanding in our culture about the nature of real love. Take a second to think of all the different contexts in which this word *love* is used. I *love* my wife; I *love* my kids; I *love* my dog; I still *love* the Beatles; and sometimes I even *love* my car. The word love has become almost meaningless because we fail to distinguish between the different states of mind and emotion to which we attach this little four-letter word.

If you want a solid definition of love as it relates to marriage, you need to go back to the divine blueprint. In Greek, the language of the New Testament, a variety of words were used to communicate the series of ideas for which we use the word *love*. Three of these words must be combined to develop a holistic understanding of real love.

Eros

The first of those Greek words is *eros*, from which our English word *erotic* is derived. This word was used to express the physical attraction that occurs between a man and a woman. Love has a physical dimension. Much of the American myth of love is rooted in the sensual or sexual dimension of love.

God is the author and creator of this dimension of love. In the proper context, sexuality is not only important but good. As a matter of fact, in the proper context it is great! God designed us to be male and female. He built into the very fabric of our beings the biological drives that attract us to the opposite sex. Those of us who are already married would probably have to honestly admit that our initial attraction to our mates was not based on some deep spiritual quality we discerned in our beloved; we simply liked the way he or she looked and felt a strange biochemical process stirring within.

Eros does have its problems, though. It is an inadequate type of love on which to build a lasting relationship. If this is the only dimension of love present in a relationship, the relationship will be shallow and one-dimensional. *Eros* comes and *eros* goes.

Eros is fickle and fading. *Eros* by itself can also get us into a lot of trouble. Some days, I just won't feel this kind of love for my mate. This lack of attraction is enough of a problem by itself, but it is compounded when I don't feel *eros* for my mate—but I do feel it for someone else's mate. In such cases, *eros* can lead to big problems!

Someone referred to *eros* as the "I love you if . . ." kind of love. It is conditional and requires the willingness and ability of the other person to give me something that gratifies the sexual side of my nature. *Eros* can never make love last. Something more is needed.

Phileo

The emotional dimension of love was expressed by the Greek word *phileo*. *Phileo* referred to the feeling component of love. When we find ourselves emotionally attracted to someone because of some attractive quality in that person, we are experiencing *phileo*. "Falling in love" is most often a mix of *eros* and *phileo*.

Anyone who has had the experience of "falling in love" knows how wonderful it is. It is wonderful when this feeling of love toward another person is reciprocated. Almost every song, movie, and television program in popular culture glorifies the *phileo* experience. Much of our cultural concept of love is rooted in this feeling. Someone has called this the "I love you because of . . ." kind of love. It is conditional and requires the ongoing process of something in the one loved still creating these feelings.

However, the *phileo* dimension of love also has serious limitations. *Phileo* is an inadequate basis on which to build a lasting relationship. Emotions are both wonderful and terrible.

Our emotional capability is a God-given gift. When emotions are operating according to God's plan, they can be great. But this side of Eden, our emotions tend to have a life of their own. Emotions are incredibly unpredictable.

I wake up one morning with wonderfully warm and loving feelings toward my wife; the very next morning, I wake up with no such feelings at all. I might even wake up with powerfully negative feelings toward my wife. If I am living my life in a way that allows my feelings to dictate my behavior, I am certain to run into problems.

Most relationships (particularly marriages) go through a series of stages. Romantic relationships begin with a period of enchantment often called "the honeymoon stage." This is the stage where both *eros* and *phileo* are in full swing. Two people have "fallen in love." They can't seem to live without each other. They find no flaw in one another. They are floating along on cloud nine. Unfortunately, this stage usually doesn't last very long.

The end of the honeymoon stage used to begin the morning after the wedding when, for the first time, the couple saw each other first thing in the morning. Both discovered that their beloved's "natural beauty" was actually a product of "better living through chemistry." Puppy love encountered doggy breath. Reality set in.

The hard realities of living together move a relationship into the second stage. This is the stage of disenchantment. Different relationships will take different lengths of time to arrive at this stage, and the arrival will be characterized by different levels of intensity. Entering the disenchantment stage will often lead to a crisis.

Suddenly, at the feeling level, Mr. Right has become Mr. Wrong. The focus shifts from the half-full glass to the half-empty glass. Each partner in the marriage discovers a series of irritating habits and behaviors about the other. Sexual attraction begins to fade. At this point, the relationship is about to reach a major crossroad. A decision will be made whether to abandon the relationship or take whatever actions are necessary to move the relationship into the third stage—the stage of maturity. The answer to the question, "How do you make love last?" is to be found in the third dimension of real love.

Stages of Marriage

Honeymoon stage   Disenchantment   Maturity

In recent years, the whole arena of romantic love has been attracting the attention of the scientific community. Biochemists have now discovered that the feelings and drives associated with romance have definite chemical components. Amazingly, scientists have been able to isolate the chemical produced by the body that stimulates the brain with feelings of passion and romance. The chemical is called phenylethylamine, or PEA for short.

Along with discovering what has been called "the chemistry of love," these same scientists have discovered some amazing facts about this chemical process. It appears that in most cases the human biochemical system can only sustain the production of PEA for a period of four years. Biochemically speaking, romantic love has its limitations.

Working with cultural anthropologists, these scientists surveyed sixty-five different cultures and found that the peak divorce rate occurred in the fourth year of marriage. Romantic feelings fade. Something more is needed to sustain a relationship and make love last.

Agape

The good news is that something more is possible. The third dimension of love is identified by use of the Greek word *agape*. This is the Greek word used most frequently in the Bible to describe the kind of love God expresses toward humanity. *Agape* is quite different from the other two types of love.

The three types of love correspond to the three-dimensional nature of man. *Eros* is a physically based love that originates in the physical dimension of man's nature. *Phileo* is an emotionally based product of the intellectual and feeling dynamics of the soul. *Agape* is a spiritually based love that has its source in our relationship with God.

Three-Dimensions and Three Loves

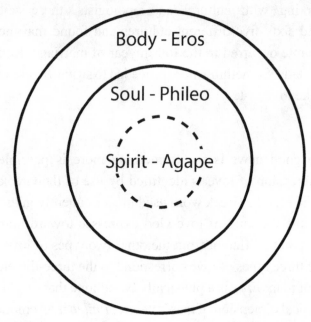

Both *eros* and *phileo* are natural in their origins and expression. *Agape* is supernatural. It is a product of the work of God's Spirit in our lives. In the last chapter, you were challenged to ask Jesus Christ to come into your life. In the moment that commitment was made you were enabled to love in a new way. With Christ in our lives we are no longer limited to the American myth of sexual and emotional love. To those very good dimensions of love a third and vital dimension has been added: *agape*. *Agape* love is the primary ingredient in a mature and lasting relationship.

Agape love is unconditional. Both *eros* and *phileo* have conditions attached to their expression; they are dependent upon the fulfillment of certain conditions in order for love to continue. *Eros* loves if the loved one gives sexual gratification and remains sexually attractive. *Phileo* loves because of certain lovable traits and characteristics in the loved one; it continues to love as long as those characteristics are present and are creating positive feelings in the lover's emotional system.

But *agape* loves in spite of flaws and inconsistencies. It has been referred to as the "I love you in spite of . . ." kind of love. It is unconditionally rooted in the nature of the lover. God's love is like this. It is rooted in his nature, not our lovability. Because Christ now lives in me, I have the ability to love in this same kind of way. *Agape* is also volitional. We now have the ability to choose to love even if we are not feeling the emotion we call love. Real love is much more than a feeling. It is a series of actions we choose to take. Real love is a commitment to seek the highest welfare of the person we choose to love. When we choose to love our beloved through periods of disenchantment and crisis we will move into the maturity stage of the marriage. To make love last requires a special kind of love. Only mature love lasts; it must be three-dimensional. *Agape* must be present and dominant.

The Work of Marriage

"Here's a little (tale) 'bout Jack and Diane." These are paraphrased words that constitute the opening line of John Mellencamp's song, "Jack and Diane." The song is an insightful look at the "all-American" love story. High school sweethearts, living in the heartland of America, are passionately in love. They graduate, marry, and head off on their honeymoon. Then, as Mellencamp observes, "life goes on." Passions fade, reality sets in, life gets tough, and "love" grows cold. The conclusion of the song is often the tragic truth: "Oh yeah, life goes on; long after the thrill of living is gone."

It appears that like millions of teens around our nation and our world, Jack and Diane never learned how to make love last. They entered marriage without anyone explaining the work of love to them.

There are a wide variety of marriages in the world today. There are marriages that end in divorce (almost fifty percent of American marriages end this way). There are marriages where the partners stay together, but the relationship is incredibly dysfunctional. There are marriages that exist in a state of peaceful coexistence but where very little love is expressed physically, emotionally, or spiritually. Then there are those few marriages where both partners are actually happy and fulfilled in the relationship. These marriages are the ones that are experiencing a nearly mystical quality that the Bible calls "oneness." (Gen. 2:18–24)

Attaining oneness takes work. When we commit to making our marriages a priority, we commit ourselves to investing the time, energy, and resources necessary for our marriages to become all that God intended them to be. When God designed the marriage relationship, he saw that it was not good for man to be alone. He created woman. He brought the man and woman together and told them that the two were to become one. The formula looks a little crazy: One becomes two in order that the two might become one.

Oneness in marriage is an expression of *agape* love. God created marriage, in part, to teach people how to love one another. We could think of marriage as a love laboratory. We certainly can learn to love in other contexts. Those who find themselves in the state of singleness don't have to think that if they are not married, they will never learn to love. But for those of us who are married, our marriages provide opportunities to learn the most important lesson we can ever learn in life. The work of moving toward oneness in marriage is a labor of love. In the work of learning to become one, we will have to learn how to love unconditionally.

I have developed an image of this task of creating oneness, which has helped me sort through immature and childish ideas about love and develop a more mature understanding of real love. I picture the husband and wife as two very unique and different gears. Ultimately, these two gears are intended to come together and "mesh" physically, emotionally, and spiritually. The meshing of the gears will then produce something that neither gear has the ability to produce by itself. The simplest and most obvious illustration of this principle is the product of our physical meshing. When we mesh physically we produce children. Most of us are pretty good at this kind of meshing. It is emotional and spiritual meshing that cause us problems.

Around the age of eighteen to twenty, we reach a level of physical maturity. Many of us begin to think about getting married and starting a family. For most, our physical maturity is not matched by emotional and spiritual maturity. Most of us are immature when we marry, and we usually marry someone who is also immature.

Immature people often have immature expectations of marriage. We bring into our marriages certain expectations (usually unconscious) of what a perfect mate should be. For men, this ideal mate is some mix of Charlize Theron, Mother Teresa, and Martha Stewart. For women, the composite may be Brad Pitt, St. Francis of Assisi, and Bill Gates. The underlying formula is relatively simple: *The ideal mate meets all my needs.*

Having formulated this ideal over the years, we then do a very cruel thing. We project this ideal, with all its expectations, onto our new mate. In most cases, my real mate will probably fail to live up to this ideal. My unconscious goal to have all my needs met will get blocked. This will produce a whole series of emotional responses ranging from anger to frustration to depression to discouragement. In other words, I will become disenchanted. This disenchantment manifests itself in an immature person's mind in the form of the thought, "Something is wrong with him (or her)."

When this process begins to happen in the life of a person who has committed themselves to God's relational priorities, it becomes an opportunity to use *agape* love to move the relationship (and the person) to a new level of maturity. What does the introduction of *agape* into this formula look like?

Agape love is self-sacrificial. It is the diametrical opposite of immature love. If I exercise *agape* love, I will no longer think my husband or wife exists to meet my needs. Marriage becomes a commitment on my part to meet their needs. The classic text that defines *agape* love is found in 1 Corinthians, Chapter 13. This text says *agape* is not self-seeking. (v. 5) Whenever my actions toward my wife reveal self-centeredness, I am not loving with *agape* love. At some point, my needs will be in conflict with my spouse's needs. When I am letting Christ live in and through me (which is the secret of releasing *agape* in my life), I will focus on serving my spouse's needs rather than my own.

Paradoxically, since my greatest needs are for security and significance, loving my mate this way will usually produce responses in my mate that will actually meet my needs in a way an egocentric approach to marriage never could. Once again, it is in losing myself for the sake of Christ and serving instead of seeking to be served, that my own needs are met.

Agape is also accepting. It attempts to know and understand my partner and her needs. *Agape* enables me to accept my mate without constantly attempting to change them. Mature love (or maybe I should say a mature person) has the ability to recognize faulty expectations and perceptions.

I find that the number one false idea in the minds of most people who are struggling with their marriages is their mate needs to change in order for their marital problems to disappear. This is a tragic lie that not only demeans the mate but also robs the spouse of discovering the value of his or her mate's uniqueness—which is a gift of God to meet their own deepest needs.

Finally, *agape* is self-critical in a positive sense. Instead of focusing on what I think is wrong with my mate, I recognize that the failure of our gears to mesh might be an indication that a few teeth on my own gears need work. Disenchantment, and the conflict or crisis produced by it, leads me to submit myself to God's transforming work in my own life. This process of growth is one of the great benefits of the marriage relationship.

Building a good marriage takes hard work. It takes hard work because marriage is the relationship where the raging monster of self most often raises its ugly head. It is a relationship where the hurt and wounded child of one's past will most frequently make his unexpected and unwanted appearance. It is a relationship where the tendency to ascend the throne of ego and demand to be served most frequently surfaces. Therefore, it is a relationship that provides great possibilities for making hearty strides in our growth toward maturity. For those of us who give our marriages their proper sense of priority, marriage provides a tremendous opportunity to learn to love and serve.

Building a Healthy Marriage

Many excellent books have been written on the subject of marriage. Rather than attempting to exhaustively deal with the subject, I would like to give you a few hints of how Allison and I tried to make our marriage a priority.

Commitment

Around the seven-year mark in our marriage, Allison and I entered a period of major disenchantment that led to a crisis. Small, unresolved issues in our relationship had been building for years. Allison began to experience severe bouts of depression, which she believed were my fault. I was experiencing unbearable frustration with her. The building tension between us reached a climax on Thanksgiving Day. What should have been a minor conflict escalated into a major crisis. By the end of the day, we both knew if something didn't change we were headed for divorce.

God often graciously intervenes in our lives when we least expect it and certainly don't deserve it. Such was the case in our lives. Instead of making a foolish decision, we made a wise (and I believe gracious in the truest sense of the word) choice. We decided we could not solve our problems by ourselves. We came to the mutual decision to seek professional help. That was one of the most difficult decisions I ever made. It started a process of professional counseling that was equally difficult. The counseling process lasted four years.

During those four years, there were many occasions when each of us felt like throwing in the towel. There were many times when we were convinced our marriage was never going to work. There were days when the most exotic forms of torture known to man seemed preferable to staying married. Through all of those difficult times, it was raw commitment that provided the glue that kept our marriage together. Commitment provided the time we needed to work through serious disenchantment and move into a new level of love and maturity in our marriage.

Since relationships often run in cycles, I can promise you that was not the last of our crisis. But we continued to work through the tough times and build a marriage that lasted. We not only committed to staying in the relationship, we committed to making the relationship as much like God's design as possible. It is hard enough to simply stay together, but staying together was not our only goal. We wanted to have a good marriage. That commitment required time, energy, and resources. As I wrote in the Introduction, Allison passed away on April 3, 2019. I cared for her at home for over five years until her Alzheimer's reached the point where she needed more care than I could give her. We were married for forty-five years. Those forty-five years were the product of God's grace, and our commitment to work hard and give our marriage the place of priority it deserved.

Communication

In order for our marriages to grow and thrive, we need to learn to communicate effectively. If commitment is the foundation of a lasting relationship, then communication provides the framework. Communication has been called the lifeblood of relationships.

Marriage was designed to be a life-sharing experience. Communication is how we share our lives. Communication doesn't occur without time spent together. Many couples have found that establishing a time on weekly basis where they can be together and enjoy each other is crucial. Think of it as a date night. The kind of planning and action we take during dating is just as valuable when we are married.

Before Allison's illness, our date nights were often spent going to a movie and out to dinner. These were times when we made sure we were in touch with what was going on in each other's lives and in our marriage. They were also times of simply having fun and enjoying one another.

At other times during the week, we might have needed to work through issues that were creating problems in our relationship. Most couples have a tendency to let little issues build until they lose perspective. They might tend to let things slide because they hate conflict. Talking through areas and issues of conflict has a way of diffusing them. Communication is a critical component in the building of a healthy marriage.

For many men, the communication component does not come easily. Wives often want to share their deepest feelings; many men, have been programmed to be relatively out of touch with their feelings. The ability to communicate at a feeling level often has to be learned with the help of a professional. I promise you, the value of spending time and resources to improve your communication skills is well worth the cost.

Caring

In a world that couldn't care less, marriage was designed to be a relationship where two people couldn't care more. Perhaps no other ingredient, except a lot of grace, is more essential in building a healthy marriage than a commitment to care.

I was a great fan of Mother Teresa. Every time I read an article about her or saw an account of what she was doing, I found myself tremendously challenged. Early in our marriage, I was reading a short biography of her life and work by British author Malcolm Muggeridge. I was so overwhelmed by the beauty of her life of service that I made a decision. I decided the real action was in Calcutta. I decided to really live the Christian life, I needed to go to India to serve the poorest of the poor with Mother Teresa.

I happened to be standing in the kitchen at the time I had this great idea. I had what I believe was an encounter with God. Although his voice was not audible, I had as strong an impression in my mind as if an audible voice had spoken. I "heard" God say, "Look around you. You don't need to go to Calcutta. You can do what Mother Teresa does right in your home."

At the time, our daughter, Stephanie, was still in diapers. Moms with small kids have one of the toughest jobs in the world! On this particular day, Allison had not had time to even think about doing the dishes. I was ready to head to Calcutta to love lepers, but I had neglected to care enough to clean the kitchen. In the spirit of Mother Teresa, I did the dishes!

Mother Teresa often explains her work on the basis of Jesus' teaching that whatever we do for one of the least of our brothers we do for Christ. (Matt. 25:40) When she sees a dying person, a leper on the street, or an unwanted child, she thinks, "There is Jesus in a distressing disguise." The day after my "revelation," I happened to be upstairs in my daughter's room when she had a monumental experience of filling her diaper. I looked at her and thought, "There is Jesus in a distressing disguise." It is hard to explain, but somehow I had a bit more joy in changing that diaper.

Marriage is a relationship that thrives on caring. I confess that I have light-years to go in this area myself. I am much more eager to be served than to serve. But I have observed over the years that the quality of my relationship with my wife was usually a direct reflection of how I was working out the caring commitment. Her Alzheimer's disease challenged me in this area in a way I never expected. When I care, I am loving with *agape* love. When I serve, I am expressing the spirit of Christ. The purpose of life is to love and to serve. Marriage is a love laboratory where God wants to teach us and bless us if we will give our marriages their proper place of priority within God's divine blueprint.

Personal Reflection

If we are married, there is no area of our lives that provides more fertile soil for assessment and adjustment than our relationships with our mates. Here are a few suggestions for putting the ideas contained in this chapter into practice:

- Find a copy of your marriage vows and read them carefully.
- Evaluate the strength of each type of love in your marriage.
- Read 1 Corinthians 13 every day for a month.
- Pray about what "gears" in your life God might want to change.
- Schedule a date night with your spouse this week.
- If your marriage is in trouble, get help!

CHAPTER EIGHT

Buy a Harley!

(and Other Tips on Parenting)

Wednesday morning, April 9, 1986, an article appeared in the *Rocky Mountain News* entitled "Rewards of Fatherhood Often Discovered Too Late." The author of the article related the story of how he responded to a friend's complaint about his wife "nagging" him to spend more time with their kids. The writer shared how he wanted to "punch his buddy right between the eyes" but didn't. He observed that some lessons could only be learned the hard way.

The columnist went on to reflect on his own failure as a father. He had found it hard to take time to give his kids a bath or wrestle on the floor with them. He shared, with painful honesty, about his reluctance to break away from watching a ball game to read them a bedtime story. Before he knew it, his children were grown and able to bathe themselves. They stopped wanting to wrestle on the floor. The time came when they were much too grown up to have Dad read them a bedtime story. That's when the fact hit him, "right between the eyes," that the rewards of fatherhood are often discovered too late!

That article held special significance for me. At five-thirty on that Wednesday morning, just about the time the newspaper containing that article was landing in the driveway of our home, a brand-new, bouncing baby boy by the name of Baker Theodore Beltz was born. I felt like the timing of the article was a message from God. I clipped the article and put it in my file labeled "Dads" to serve as a constant reminder that my children are a gift of God, intended to be a vital priority in my relational network.

I suppose many people have had memorable New Year's Eves. There is one I will never forget. At about eleven-thirty on the morning of December 31, 1979, my very pregnant wife began to have contractions. The contractions progressed mildly throughout the day. That evening, as the contractions grew closer together and more intense, we packed our little car and headed toward Rose Hospital. While the rest of the world was watching the crowds gathered in Times Square, we were heavy into Lamaze breathing techniques. Shortly after the clock struck twelve, we headed toward the delivery room. Early in the morning of the first day of a new decade, our daughter, Stephanie, was born. I still vividly remember holding my precious little girl in my arms, wondering what she needed from me and what it meant to be a dad.

It seems like only yesterday, and yet as I write these words, that little "baby" is a mother herself. And I'm now a grandfather! Over the years, the challenges and rewards of fatherhood have been a major part of living out the divine blueprint in my own life. The birth of Baker more than doubled the challenges and exponentially increased the rewards. Through these years I have learned some of the answers to those critical questions I wondered about on that New Year's Day so long ago.

The Primary Task of Fathering

I remember walking out of the hospital that cold and snowy New Year's Day and heading for my car to drive home. As I began to cross the street, the strangest thought entered my mind. Without warning, the words "life insurance" popped onto the screen of my consciousness. I don't believe I had ever given life insurance a thought before that moment. But now I was a dad. What do dads do? They are providers and protectors; *ergo*, life insurance.

Although providing and protecting are two of my responsibilities as a father, neither of those responsibilities is my primary task in the divine blueprint. My primary task as a parent who takes his marching orders from God is to bless my children. I am to be the human vehicle through whom God touches the lives of my children with a powerful spiritual reality that produces spiritual empowerment and emotional wholeness in their lives.

In the patriarchal society of ancient Israel, this experience of blessing was to be transmitted from father to son, generation to generation. Genesis, Chapter 12 relates how God entered into a redemptive covenant with a man named Abraham. That covenant ultimately found fulfillment in the person and work of Jesus Christ and the gift of regeneration and transformation made possible by the indwelling presence of the Holy Spirit. God said to Abraham:

> *I will bless you. . .*
> *You will be a (source of) blessing . . .*
> *Through you all nations (humanity) will be blessed.*
> Genesis 12:1–3 (author's own translation)

This covenant was worked out by a process intimately related to the father-child relationship. The intended scenario was:

> **God blesses Abraham > Abraham becomes**
> **a blessed father > Abraham blesses his son >**
> **His son grows to become a blessed father >**
> **He blesses his son > His son grows to become**
> **a blessed father > etc.**

Obviously, something went wrong somewhere. But God's design from the beginning was that the primary job of a parent was to bless their children. What does this look like?

In their book, *The Blessing*, Gary Smalley and John Trent attempt to take this ancient concept and translate it for contemporary application. They break down the impartation of blessing into five components. For the sake of our discussion, I will synthesize the five into three: time, tenderness, and truth. They are the dynamics that must be present in our relationships with our children if we are to meet their deepest needs and fulfill our primary task as parents.

The Gift of Time

When we come to grips with the fact that life is short, we begin to realize that one of our most valuable possessions is time. Every choice I make about how I spend my day involves the use of this limited resource. Over the years, I came to understand how my children desperately needed a healthy chunk of that time.

In the Old Testament book of Deuteronomy, Moses delivered a series of messages to the people of Israel as they finally prepared to enter and possess the Promised Land. With Israel camped on the east bank of the Jordan River,

Moses issued a command that became a creedal statement for the nation. Moses said, "Hear, O Israel: The LORD our God, the LORD is one. Love the LORD your God with all your heart and with all your soul and with all your strength." (Deut. 6:4–5) This was the biblical text Jesus quoted when asked about the greatest commandment.

Although I was familiar with this command, I was surprised to see what immediately follows the command. Moses challenged the people of Israel to impress these commandments on their own hearts and then to impress them on their children. He told the parents to accomplish this task by talking about them to their children when they sat at home, when they walked along the road, when they went to bed, and when they woke up. The impartation of God's truth was not to occur in a classroom setting, but in the context of parents and their children spending quality time together. The destiny of the nation of Israel depended on it. Families were to become what Edith Schaeffer called a "relay of truth."

There is a significant difference, of course, between the culture of that day and our own. In those days, moms and dads and boys and girls spent a great deal of time together. Living in a primarily rural and agricultural society, children often worked alongside their fathers in the field or alongside their mothers in the home. Many of the distractions of our modern society didn't even exist in ancient Israel. What was the norm in ancient times must be worked at in our culture.

This challenge was illustrated for me in an article published in *Scientific American* magazine entitled "The Origins of Alienation." The article reported the results of a study involving families with preschool children. The intention of the study was to discover how much time fathers of preschool children were spending on quality interaction with their children. The fathers were first asked to estimate how much time they were spending daily with their children. The average reported response was an estimated fifteen to twenty minutes a day. This, in and of itself, seems like a small amount. But the real truth emerged as those conducting the study monitored the interaction of these fathers with their children.

The results of the study were staggering. The actual amount of time these children were being given by their fathers amounted to 2.7 encounters daily, consisting of an average cumulative elapsed time of thirty-seven seconds! Thirty-seven seconds a day during the period of development where personality, psychosexual development, and identity are at their most formative stages. Recent studies show the average preschooler in America spends twenty-five to thirty hours a week in front of a television set or ingesting visual media of some sort. In his book, *Fatherless America*, sociologist David Blankenhorn called this issue the most urgent social problem in America.

Sometimes when I remember the above passage in Deuteronomy, I think about days when I had to be at an early morning meeting and then worked straight through into the late evening. On those days, I didn't see my children awake. I had lost an entire day of influence in my children's lives and was robbed of the joy of simply enjoying them. I hated those days and I am glad that they were few and far between. Unfortunately, for some dads and their kids, days like those are the rule rather than the exception.

I also think about those days when I came home from work and just wanted to get in a fetal position and be left alone. At those times, I often remembered a line from a documentary called *The Family Gone Wild*. The film includes a scene in which a father comes home after a long day at work feeling the way I just described. His sixth-grade daughter is waiting for him in the driveway, hoping to play tetherball with her dad. Every fiber of his being wants to hit the couch and "veg out." But the father makes the observation that the principle in his life that gives him the motivation to go out and play tetherball is; "When I get home, I begin the most important work of the day."

I am one of those lucky guys who actually enjoys his job. I have spent nearly fifty years on work that is filled with significant activity. I have taught, counseled, written books, helped produce movies and television shows, and helped lead and pastor several good churches. All of those tasks were important. I also am very aware that God had the ability to raise up others who were able to perform those tasks better than I. But I was the only daddy that Baker and Stephanie had. If I failed at my job as a father, no one else could have, or would have, filled that void. The most important work of my day was to love my wife and children and to be involved in a significant way in their lives. That will only take place when there is a significant investment of time in these relationships. It takes time together with our children to bless them.

Smalley and Trent say that meaningful touch and spoken words are two of the components necessary to give our children the blessing. One of my favorite memories with my son was the day we went to the Promisekeepers National Men's Conference in Boulder, Colorado.

It was a beautiful Saturday morning in Colorado, and my son and I decided to ride to the conference on my Harley. As Baker held on for dear life, the words "meaningful touch" took on a whole new spin. We rode and talked and went to the conference. After the morning session, we rode into the mountains to have lunch at a small cafe. On the way back to Denver, we stopped and walked along a railroad track, waiting to watch trains while my son hunted for "hidden treasure." It was an entire day of talk and touch and time together. I was blessing my son.

The Gift of Tenderness

There is nothing magical about time spent with our children, in and of itself. What is important is what goes on during that time. Sitting in the same room with our children while we all watch television might be enjoyable, but it is rarely what you could call quality time.

One of the classic biblical texts on parenting is found in the New Testament Book of Ephesians. In the sixth chapter of this little epistle, the apostle Paul instructs us to raise our children "in the training and instruction of the Lord." (Eph. 6:4) The word in the Greek text that is translated "raise them up" or "bring them up" is the word *ektrepho*. This word means "to nurture or to nourish." It implies an attitude of care, provision, and support.

Nurture is the care and tenderness given to a person for the purpose of facilitating his or her health and growth.

Dr. Ross Campbell, in his excellent book *How to Really Love Your Child*, gives several suggestions about how to build nurturing relationships. Dr. Campbell says that in order to have quality time with our children, we must work at giving focused attention. The most basic characteristic of focused attention is eye contact. It always amazed me to note the difference between just being around my children and having this kind of eyeball-to-eyeball interaction with them. My daughter taught me this lesson early in my parenting education.

I was a reasonably good early-morning person. When Stephanie was a toddler, she used to get up two or three times in the middle of the night and then arise for the day at about five-thirty in the morning. In order to survive this schedule, my wife and I struck a deal. Allison took the "night shift" and I took on early-morning duty so that she could catch up on her sleep after these frequent middle-of-the-night episodes with Stephanie. I actually looked forward to these early-morning times with my daughter. I also began to develop a little routine that ended up teaching me a lesson about focused attention.

The two essential items in my early-morning routine in those days were a cup of hot coffee and the morning paper. I would turn on a children's program on TV (educational, of course) and settle onto the couch with paper and coffee to "spend a little time with Stephanie." I even developed the skill of responding to Stephanie's many questions without losing my place in the paper.

One morning as I was going through my "Yes, Sweetie" response to one of those profound two-year-old inquiries about the nature of life and the universe, I had a startling experience.

Stephanie had figured out my game. As I was reading, suddenly the paper was ripped right out of my hand. I found myself staring right into the eyes of my beautiful little girl. The message was clear! She wanted my focused attention, not just my physical presence.

The same was true of my son when he was little. I was usually up and well into my morning routine when he woke up. I would hear him coming down the hall toward the living room. I would put down whatever I was doing and gear up for some focused attention.

Giving focused attention is a commitment to nurturing. It requires a conscious decision to enter into the world of our children. It usually means doing things that we wouldn't think of doing otherwise. For mothers, that might mean riding bikes, building forts, and playing sports with their sons (or daughters). For fathers that might mean being willing to get down on the floor and play dolls with their daughters. That might not seem very masculine, but that is what it means to be a daddy.

I recently ran across a survey called "A Good Father." A group of children had been asked to finish the sentence, "A good father . . ." The survey revealed the following list of answers:

A good father . . .

helps kids learn to ride a bike

reads stories to the kids

says "don't eat mud"

loves

explains when asked to explain

goes to church and Sunday school

is home a lot

listens

protects me

lets my friends come in to play

takes me fishing

disciplines me

helps me

spends time with me

holds me

doesn't go away

It seems kind of crazy that the things that really matter to children are so simple. They long for nurturing time from their parents, time that includes eye contact and tender touch, time when we leave the adult world and enter the world of children, time sitting on the floor playing with trucks and dolls.

Nurturing also involves the messages we send our children both verbally and nonverbally. I remember when my daughter was a teenager. Over the years, I had attempted to affirm her by speaking words that expressed how much I valued her. When she reached adolescence, I became aware of how much of my interaction with her was critical and negative. I began to wonder how I could be more affirming.

At the time, I did much of my studying and writing in my office at home. This office happened to be located next to Stephanie's bedroom. Stephanie loved to come into the office when I wasn't around to tinker with my computer and use my phone. These were the days before children had their own laptops and smart phones.

I had a program on the computer called After Dark. This program was a screen saver that automatically put the computer to sleep and put moving objects on the screen. I had flying toasters, colorful fish, shooting stars, and a whole host of options on this program. One of the options allowed you to put messages on the screen that repeatedly floated across the monitor in a variety of colors. Stephanie and I began to use this program as a high-tech vehicle of communication. I would put a message on the screen, such as "Stephanie: a young woman of sterling character and graceful bearing."

I would return home to find the following on the screen: "Yuk! Gag me with a spoon!"

One day, I decided to get both theological and etymological. I put the following message on the screen: "Stephanie; from the Greek *stephanos*, meaning crowned one; i.e., queen or princess." I was convinced that Stephanie would be blessed by such a thoughtful and scholarly electronic affirmation.

When I came home that evening, I found Stephanie's response: "Old men like you lose their hair and buy big toys to make up for it!"

I didn't say this would be easy! But if we can keep working at being nurturing, we hopefully give our children two priceless gifts. The first is the gift of a positive, biblical sense of self-esteem. There can be little doubt that the quality of our children's lives will be directly related to self-esteem. This gift is a direct product of the quality of nurturing time we give them.

Many of us lacked this kind of nurture growing up. We have paid the price for this deficiency both emotionally and relationally. We were not blessed. Growing up in non-nurturing families, we developed either low self-esteem or no self-esteem. Much of our unconscious motivations in adult life are attempts to prove that we are valuable. We must remember that we are the products of products.

As the Bible reminds us, the sins of the fathers have been visited on the children. But we have a chance to break the cycle. If as parents, we can simply make a difference in this area of nurturing and build self-esteem into our children, then they will experience a quality of life much more positive than we experienced. And we hope (and pray) they will continue this process in the nurturing of their children. We can thereby set in motion a positive pattern of quality nurturing that will bear fruit for generations to come.

The Gift of Truth

The greatest gift we can give our children is a vital and healthy relationship with God. One of the most important hours in our house used to begin around eight o'clock each evening. That was the time when we began the process (or should I say battle?) of getting our children into bed. It was also the time when we tried to have a period of focused spiritual input in their lives.

As the father in our home, I believed God had given me a unique role in bringing spiritual blessing to my children. I longed to lead them into a vital and positive relationship with God. I knew that at some point there would be personal decisions they would have to make on their own. I also knew that what happened in our home in those early years would lay a foundation on which those later decisions would be based.

When Stephanie was born, I began a very simple ritual every night. The final encounter of my day with her was to hold her in my arms and pray for her. I would always end my prayer by praying over her the Levitical blessing found in the Old Testament Book of Numbers:

> *The LORD bless you and keep you;*
>
> *the LORD make his face shine upon you*
>
> *and be gracious to you;*
>
> *the LORD lift up the light of his countenance*
>
> *upon you and give you peace.* (Numbers 6:24–26)

God gave this prayer to the priesthood of Israel to bless the nation. As the "priest" of my family, I used it to ask the Lord to bless my children.

In addition to praying for Stephanie, Allison and I would rock her and sing spiritual songs of praise and worship. We wanted to fill her little mind and spirit with positive input as she drifted off to sleep each night. As she grew older, we read to her the normal stories of childhood, including stories about God's love for her. Above all else, I wanted to impart to her a positive image of God as the one, who above all others, loved her and cared for her.

When Baker came along, the challenge doubled. Each of our children is so unique that we need to find the vehicle of truth that is most effective with him or her. Baker loved to listen to Bible stories. He wouldn't go to sleep at night until both Mom and Dad had prayed for him. I always ended my prayers for him as I did with Stephanie by praying over him the Levitical blessing out of Numbers.

When I think back on those questions I asked the day Stephanie was born, I realize that part of what our children need from us is the gift of truth. The family is a "relay of truth." The impartation and modeling of life-changing and life-shaping truth is the job of the family.

I recently attended my fiftieth high school class reunion. When I was in high school, I ran on our school track team. Going through my old yearbook before the reunion, I was reminded that I was a member of several relay teams. The critical seconds in a relay race involve the few short feet when one runner passes the baton to the next runner. Our team often won races against much faster teams because we won the race on the precision of the baton transfer. Other times, we lost races against teams with slower runners by fumbling the baton in the handoff.

Life is like a relay race. God has handed us the baton of truth. He has entrusted us with the lives of our children and instructed us to pass the baton. Part of that exchange will involve verbal instruction. Part of that exchange will involve the process of discipline. Most of the exchange will be a matter of prayer and example. Our children will learn what they live. Giving our children the gift of truth will require the ongoing discipline of working the truth out in our own lives.

Every once in a while, we have an experience that lets us know how the "race" is going. One of my favorites took place one morning when Baker was about five, and I was having my morning time of prayer and Bible study in what was my favorite chair in the living room. It was an old overstuffed easy chair that I had recovered in fake black and white cowhide. In the house we lived in at the time, it sat next to a restored 1953 Seeburg jukebox, just like the one in *Happy Days*. We also had an old Coke machine in one corner of the living room, and thanks to ground level sliding doors, I kept my Harley-Davidson motorcycle in the other corner. (A couple of years later, and in a different house, I was able to add a fully restored Texaco gas pump to the decor!) This environment was highlighted by one wall of the living room that was all glass and looked out on a perfect view of the front range of the Rocky Mountains. This was the spot where I did my best praying, thinking, and writing.

On this particular morning, I had finished praying and was working on a book I was writing. Baker came running into the living room as soon as he awoke. We were in a stretch where the first thing he wanted to do in the morning was climb up in my lap and sit for a while. I took full advantage of this special period of grace!

Seeing me writing, Baker stopped and asked why I was working. I replied that I had not finished the work I needed to do the day before. He asked, "Are you not finished because I sat too long on your lap?" I saw an opportunity to use his question to affirm my love for him and his value to me, so I answered, "Nothing in the whole world is more important than you sitting on my lap."

I saw a grin spread across his face as he said, "That's wrong, Dad."

I was stunned, so I asked, "What do you mean?"

Baker replied, "God is more important, Dad!"

Pretty good theology for a five-year-old! I had an idea of how I could use this reply to teach him another lesson, so I said, "Baker, do you know how Daddy likes to sit in this chair each morning and read his Bible and pray?" Baker shook his head in the affirmative. "Well, that's kind of like Dad sitting in God's lap," I said.

Baker smiled broadly and exclaimed, "Cool, Dad!" That little encounter was a huge affirmation that the gift of truth was taking root in his life. That little guy is now thirty-three and one of my favorite people on the planet.

Like it or not, many of our children's unconscious ideas and feelings about a heavenly Father will be shaped and influenced by their experience of their earthly father. I'm sure that at the age of five, Baker envisioned God as some kind of giant, blown-up version of me. Therefore, our own relationship with God needs to be vital and positive if we are effectively going to give to give our children the gift of truth.

Time, tenderness, and truth: three gifts that our children desperately need. Gifts that, when given with consistency, produce in the lives of our children the spiritual reality the Bible calls "the blessing." These three gifts have the potential of facilitating in our children's lives the two most significant qualities we can impart as parents—a positive and healthy view of God and a healthy, biblical sense of self-esteem. If we are successful in passing along these gifts, we will have helped our children begin, at an early age, to live according to the divine blueprint and avoid many of the pitfalls that come with getting hooked into the Solomon Syndrome.

Personal Reflection

Here are a few questions to think about and ideas to try in your effort to build this priority on your pyramid:

- Monitor your time with your kids this week; how much time are you investing in your children on a daily basis?
- Are you giving your children focused attention?
- Work on practicing eye contact and gentle touch with your kids.
- Pray with your children before they go to bed this week. Touch their heads gently and ask God to bless them.
- Plan a fun outing this weekend.
- Go to church as a family.

CHAPTER NINE

Hanging Out at Grace's Place

(Reflections on the Subject of Friends)

There was an old yellow Porsche parked in my girlfriend's driveway. Actually, the driveway technically belonged to a former girlfriend, whom I still had an immense crush on. The year was 1970, and I was home from college on spring break. The presence of the Porsche confirmed the rumors.

For several years, I had been wrestling with the issue of what life was all about. Like many of my contemporaries, I was looking for answers in some very strange places. I had listened to the voices that criticized the shallow materialism of the establishment and that advocated drugs, sex, and rock and roll as the pathway to freedom and meaning. My former girlfriend,

Sydna, had enough intelligence to analyze the changes taking place in my life and tell me to get lost.

Then I began to hear the stories. Some of my old school friends had become "Jesus freaks." I probably wouldn't have paid much attention to the rumors except that my old flame was part of the group. Not only had she become a Christian (I had no idea what this even meant at the time), she was actually dating the youth minister who was leading this new religious movement so many of my old schoolmates were caught up in. His name was Richard Beach. The Porsche was his, and so was my old girlfriend!

I finally met Rich on the Fourth of July, 1970. I was with a group of friends who had gone to a party at an abandoned rock quarry outside Kansas City. It was a notorious hangout for the "turn on, tune in, and drop out" crowd. Upon arriving at the quarry, I was delighted to see a rock band, complete with generators, ready to crank up the tunes. It looked like it was going to be a great afternoon. Then I saw them—the Jesus freaks. It was a setup! The band was with them and so was my old girlfriend.

Everyone gathered around to hear the band play. When the band finished, Rich stood and addressed the crowd. He talked about Jesus Christ. He also told the crowd that a couple of the people with him wanted to tell us what Christ meant in their lives. I distinctly remember two of the people who shared their stories that afternoon. One was a fellow by the name of Bud Abel. Bud had recently retired from his career as an outside linebacker for the Kansas City Chiefs. His presence and story quickly silenced any would-be hecklers in the crowd. Even though I was feeling a little rowdy myself, I decided to be on my best behavior.

After Bud finished, Rich introduced Sydna. She stood in front of this crowd and told how Jesus Christ had changed her life. I can't remember much of what she said, but I remember thinking she looked about as cute as it was possible for a girl to look. It really bugged me that she was dating this guy Rich instead of me.

When Sydna finished speaking, Rich rose again and explained how it was possible to have a personal relationship with Jesus Christ. He invited anyone who wanted to talk further to stick around for a while. I saw my opportunity. I wasn't buying into this Jesus stuff for a minute, but I thought that with my arsenal of arguments, finely honed from a semester of college philosophy, it might be my chance to win back Sydna's affection.

For the next forty-five minutes, it was the Christians against the lions! I certainly wish someone had taped that discussion. I tried to baffle Rich with lofty philosophical arguments; he responded with brief but kind responses, always punctuated with a verse from the Bible. I wasn't always able to figure out how his response fit my argument. Later, I decided that he was attempting to plant spiritual seeds in my life hoping that they might bear fruit at some later time.

When our discussion was finished, we shook hands. Rich told me that God loved me and that he did, too. I thought at the time that this was a pretty strange thing for one guy to say to another guy. All I could manage to say in response was a shallow and meaningless "I love you, too."

I didn't convince Rich to give up his Christian faith, and I didn't convince Sydna to give up Rich. I actually left the rock quarry feeling like I had done a pretty good job of making Rich's faith look foolish. I had no idea that by the time the next

Fourth of July rolled around, Rich Beach would become the best friend I had ever had.

Over the next few months my life went great. I moved into a slick apartment with one of my best friends. I was doing well in my work at the university. I was dating some of the cutest girls in school. I had a nice new Volkswagen bug with a great stereo. I couldn't have written a better script for my life. There was only one problem; it wasn't working. I still felt an emptiness and restlessness inside. My life lacked an adequate sense of meaning, purpose, and direction. Something was missing.

By the fall of that year, I decided I had to figure this out once and for all. I decided every weekend I would visit a different church, synagogue, mosque, or temple until I knew whether or not there was a valid spiritual dimension to life. My first visit proved "fatal." I visited the church where Rich, Sydna, Bud, and the other folks from the rock quarry attended. The pastor was a great guy by the name of Ted Nissen. I had met Ted before when he was visiting our high school to see some of the students who attended Colonial Presbyterian Church. I thought that going to hear Ted speak was a logical place to begin my pilgrimage. I also thought it might give me a chance to sneak another peek at Sydna. My plan was to sit in the back of church and cruise out the door as soon as the service was over. I didn't want any of the gang from the rock quarry to know I was there. The plan was foiled by one of my former wrestling teammates from high school. Bob spotted me and sat next to me in the service. He also invited me to come out and play football with the church team the following Saturday. I told him I would try, even though eight o'clock on a Saturday morning seemed a bit difficult to make, given the events I had planned for Friday night.

Nonetheless, the following Saturday I showed up to play football with the Colonial team against another church team. During the game, a fight broke out between the two church groups. I found myself looking at all these guys rolling around on the ground wrestling with each other. I remember saying to myself, "I think I could be a Christian!"

That morning was the beginning of a relationship with a group of young men that eventually led me to start attending a Bible study for college students. At the study, I continued to hear about the difference between man's attempts at being religious (which was my concept of what it meant to be a Christian) and a real relationship with Jesus Christ.

By the second week of November, I had thought a great deal about what it would mean to commit my life to Jesus Christ. I had started to count the cost. I knew that much of my lifestyle was inconsistent with what Christ would want for my life. I knew that I would have to make, or allow Christ to make, big changes in my ethical and moral conduct. I knew I would have to give up "altering my state of consciousness" and change much of my dating behavior. I thought I could handle most of that. My biggest worry was the fear that I would probably lose all my buddies.

At first, some of my friends shared my interest in exploring spiritual things. That was still "hip" in the early seventies. As I became more serious about the claims of Christ and what they might mean for my life, my friends decided to get back to the party life. I was pretty sure a decision to receive Christ as Savior and follow him as Lord would mean losing the friendships I had developed over the years. I had no idea at the time that God would be able to fill the void created by this loss with a quality of friendship I had never before experienced.

The fateful night arrived in that second week of November. I was sitting in my room reading the Gospel of John. Suddenly and unexpectedly, truth hit me in a way it never had before. I had one of those rare moments of mental and spiritual clarity, and I knew that Jesus was who he claimed to be. I knew he lived and died for me and rose again. I knew he was alive and had the power to invade my life. I even knew that he had a plan for my life if I was willing to surrender myself to him. I vividly remember thinking, "If all this is true, nothing in all the world is more important than making this decision." I dropped to my knees at the side of the bed and began to pray. I said something like, "Lord, I have tried to run my life for twenty years, and I'm not doing a very good job of it. I really need you. Thank you for dying on the cross for me. Please come into my life, Lord Jesus." It really was that simple. He came. I know; I was there!

I don't believe it always happens this way, but for me, receiving Christ did mean the loss of many old friends. At the time, I was young and immature, and so were most of my friends. Gratefully, over the years some of those old friendships have been rekindled. But God filled that void with the gift of true friendship. A small group of Christian men began to teach me what it's like to have real friends.

Cheers!

When I think about the role friendship has played in my life since that night in 1970, I am reminded of the TV show *Cheers*. One night during the first season of the show, I happened to be walking through the family room when the theme song for the show came on the air. The words really hit home. They described a place where "everybody knows your name," a place where people share common struggles and are genuinely glad you are there.

I remember thinking how tragic it was to waste such a great song on a TV show about a bar. I thought that song should be the anthem of the church. Unfortunately, in the imperfect world in which we live, some bars may provide better fellowship than some of our churches. That is not the way it was intended to be. Fortunately, that was not my experience.

Over the years I have had the great blessing of having friends who have radically improved the quality of my life. They have taught me the true meaning of friendship. They have also helped me realize how critical the friendship rung on the ladder is in experiencing the quality of life that God intended for us. My Christian friends have challenged, encouraged, instructed, and shared the journey of living a life that counts. They have taken me to what I call "Grace's Place."

Grace's Place is a spiritual reality in which the theme song from *Cheers* finds fulfillment. It is a network of relationships that is always there when "making your way in the world today" has taken everything you've got. It is a place where a small group of men or women "know your name" and are "always glad you came." Grace's Place is a metaphor for the priority of friendship within the relational network God has designed to meet our real needs.

Seven Qualities of Authentic Friendship

The quality of relationship it takes to have a Grace's Place experience in your life is what the Bible calls fellowship. Fellowship is our English translation of the Greek word *koinonia*. *Koinonia* means "sharing in common." Authentic fellowship is a sharing of our lives with other people. Several years ago,

Louis Evans Jr., then pastor of National Presbyterian Church in Washington, D.C., wrote a book called *Creative Love*. In the book, Dr. Evans articulated the principles his church attempted to follow in what he called covenant groups. A covenant group is an organizational attempt to create authentic friendship and fellowship. The covenants to which these groups committed themselves bear a striking resemblance to the commitments John Wesley built into his class meetings during the time of the Great Awakening. If we can develop a few friendships characterized by these qualities we will be a long way toward discovering our own Grace's Place.

Quality One: Unconditional Love

If my relationship with Rich Beach taught me anything about authentic friendship, it is that an authentic friendship must be built on the foundation of unconditional love. Before meeting Rich, I had never experienced an unconditional friendship. What often pass for friendships in our culture are actually relationships of convenience and mutual usefulness. We develop these "friendships" based on what someone can do for us or how the relationship will help us get ahead in the rat race. Most of these relationships are highly conditional.

I know about these kinds of relationships. In my "misspent youth," I wanted to be friends with people who would help me look good (a difficult task at the time). I wanted to run around with the "in group" and the "cool" kids so I would be identified with them. If someone didn't measure up to my criteria in these areas, I didn't have time or energy for them.

This approach to relationships is incredibly destructive. Not only is it destructive for the person who doesn't quite measure up to our standard, it is destructive to our own inner life. It is a vivid exercise in human self-centeredness. Every time we act along these lines we reinforce negative dynamics in our inner lives. What often passes for friendship in such a scenario is simply two people using each other. My relationship with Rich was not like that.

It didn't take long for me to realize that Rich liked me for me. I had very little to offer him; I could not have improved his image or his social standing. But Rich couldn't have cared less about those kinds of things. His whole approach to our relationship was one of unconditional love. He was committed to my highest welfare and spiritual growth. He became a human vehicle through whom the unconditional love of Christ was expressed.

Rich became more than a friend. He was a spiritual mentor who helped me grow through the difficult, early years of my relationship with Christ. Sydna got away (from both of us!), but our friendship lasted through the years. On October 23, 2010, Rich lost a fifteen-year battle with prostate cancer. The loss I felt, and still feel, is impossible to explain.

Quality Two: Availability

It is a great gift to have a friend like Rich. Many people go through a whole lifetime without ever having one friend of this caliber. I have had the good fortune of having several. In the spring of 1980, I met Bo Mitchell. His friendship changed the course of my life. Bo was a successful young businessman when we met. We teamed up to develop a ministry for young businessmen and their families. For over ten years, Bo and I led men's retreats around the nation, sharing many of the principles contained in these pages.

In the early days of our friendship, Bo used to say, "Everything I have is yours, except my wife." He meant it.

If my car broke down, Bo considered it his problem. When I couldn't find a publisher for my first book, *How to Survive the End of the World*, Bo put up the money to self-publish the book. Together we became Full Court Press. When Allison and I were going through marital struggles, Bo called every day and encouraged me to "hang in there." When the idea for Cherry Hills Community Church seemed to be a calling from God, Bo put every ounce of his energy, creativity, ability, and resources into making the church a reality.

Bo taught me and modeled the covenant of availability for me. Over the years, I've tried to reciprocate in small ways. But I could never match the level of generosity and availability Bo has shown me through the years—and continues to show me to this day. When my wife needed to be moved to a memory care facility, Bo knew the expense was beyond my ability to handle for long. He went to eleven long-time friends and asked each to help, one a month, with the expense. He was the first to write a check to help. That's what authentic friendship looks like. It requires a commitment of availability of our time, energy, and resources. Few friendships develop this level of commitment.

Quality Three: Accountability

It is not easy to live according to the principles and commitments outlined in this book. It is human nature to drift toward mediocrity. We all need friends who hold us accountable and challenge us to be our best. We need friends who help us keep our belief systems, goals, and behavior on track. We need friends who love us enough to confront us when we need it. For over twenty years, Jim Dixon was that kind of a friend to me.

I moved to Colorado in 1975 to begin a master's program in biblical studies at Denver Seminary. I had met Jim at a friend's wedding in Kansas City the summer before. When we moved to Denver, I needed a place to do my seminary field ministry, so I contacted Jim.

At the time, Jim was the Director of Christian Education at Faith Presbyterian Church in Aurora, Colorado. He was willing to take a risk and let me teach an adult elective class at Faith. My teaching ministry eventually led to an internship at the church, which grew into a full-time job as Director of Adult Education.

Jim moved into the position of Associate Pastor as his own preaching gifts began to blossom. Throughout the years, I served at Faith Church, Jim was a constant source of encouragement and accountability.

In January 1982, Jim, Bo, and I began the adventure of starting a new church. On March 7, Cherry Hills Community Church opened its doors with Jim as the senior pastor and me as the teaching pastor. We worked together almost every day until I left to become the senior pastor of a church in Northern California in 1997.

During those years, we worked to hold each other accountable. When Jim was having a tough time, I knew it. I tried to be there to encourage and challenge him. When I was struggling, Jim knew it. He was always there to challenge and encourage me. When were both having a tough time, we'd go see a stupid movie together and try to encourage each other. That's what real friends are like. They hold each other accountable.

Quality Four: Honesty

Authentic accountability requires honesty. In each of the relationships I've mentioned in this chapter, there has been the common thread of a commitment to honesty. When I'm having a tough time and need someone to talk to, I know I can be honest with my friends. I tell them what is really going on in my gut and they tell me the same.

In John Wesley's class meetings, every member was required to tell the other members of the group the "true state of his soul" at least once a week. In obedience to James 5:16, they confessed their sins to one another and prayed for one another. That takes honesty.

Honesty requires hard work. Sometimes, it means confronting our friends when we sense something is not quite right. This kind of honesty can produce conflict. Superficial relationships don't handle conflict well. Authentic friendships grow through conflict. "As iron sharpens iron," the Book of Proverbs says, "so one man sharpens another." (Prov. 27:17) "The kisses of an enemy are deceitful, but faithful are the wounds of a friend." (Prov. 27:6, author's own translation)

It seems that too often Christian leaders fall into sin and lose their ministry, or at least the sense of integrity that accompanied their ministry. I have the suspicion these are men whose success has led to a degree of isolation. In isolation, no one knew what was really going on in their lives. They didn't have friends with whom they could be truly honest. That is tragic. We all need the honesty that characterizes true friendship.

Quality Five: Confidentiality

An open and honest friendship requires a high level of trust. If I am going to share my struggles with a buddy, I need to have the confidence that what I share is not going to appear as a headline in next week's *National Enquirer*.

Most people are not very good in this area of confidentiality. Nothing kills honesty in a relationship like a breach of confidence. Loose lips not only sink ships, they also sink friendships. True friends know how to keep their mouths shut and hold confidences in confidence.

Quality Six: Regularity

Friendships, like all relationships, require the investment of time and energy. The friends I have grown close to are the ones with whom I spend time. I believe the reason many people fail to develop authentic friendships is they fail to plan regular times of fellowship into their schedules.

I live in a busy metropolitan area. My life is filled with activity. I have more opportunities than time, so I have to make choices about how I spend my time. I must discipline myself not to be so busy attending to the urgent that the truly important gets neglected.

I knew that I needed regular time alone with Allison; I scheduled it. I also needed regular time with Stephanie and Baker; I planned it. But I also learned I needed regular time with a small group of men who provided me with a Grace's Place experience. It takes quality time of consistent regularity to build authentic friendships.

Quality Seven: Prayer

Authentic friends pray for one another. There is no greater gift to give a friend than intercession on their behalf in the presence of the living God. I need friends in my life who are committed to praying for me.

The last few years have been very difficult years due to my wife's illness. I have struggled. I know we live in a fallen world where bad things happen even to men and women who sincerely live godly lives. I have no reason to think that my son should not have a bi-polar disorder or my wife have Alzheimer's disease.

But knowing this does not make it easier. Often, in times like this, men and women experience a kind of special grace of God's comfort. I have not. It has impacted my confidence in God's care and made prayer difficult. But I have friends that prayed for my wife and me. I need them now more than ever. As I pray for them, and as they pray for me, our friendships deepen and grow more significant.

Proactive Friendship

Perhaps you have never had the kind of relationship characterized by the seven qualities of authentic friendship. You are not alone. I saw recently a report, which indicated that in every age group, from the Greatest Generation to Baby Boomers, to Millennials, to Generations X, Y, and Z, over forty percent reported they were lonely. It seems loneliness knows no age limitations.

You may think you could never have such a friendship. Let me assure you, you can. Such friendships can be developed. My friendships with Rich, Bo, and Jim developed naturally. I didn't have to invest a great deal of energy to make them happen. Then a strange thing occurred. I began to lose touch with them. Rich was living in another city which made consistent time together impossible. Jim and I were so busy with our different responsibilities at the church that we were rarely getting much time together. Bo had teamed up with a few other men to develop several new ministries. We were only connecting sporadically. The friendship component of my ladder was in bad shape, and I was feeling lonely and isolated.

I wish I could tell you that I was wise enough and exhibited the initiative to work on this area of need, but that is not quite how it happened. God was getting ready to teach me a lesson about how to develop intentional friendships.

Without giving much thought to the implications of my actions, I started to think about forming a discipleship group with several men I wanted to get to know better. A couple of the men were new Christians whom I thought I might be able to help in the process of their spiritual growth. I began to call them to see if they would be interested in being part of a group. Every man I asked responded enthusiastically.

We began meeting together with a commitment to meet regularly, every other week, at lunchtime on Thursdays. Our objective was to tackle a discipleship program developed by the Navigators. The 2:7 Series required a commitment to memorize Scripture, cultivate a daily discipline of Bible study and prayer, work to develop basic skills in ministry, and hold each other accountable.

As our group spent time together, an exciting chemistry evolved. Along with accomplishing the tasks to which we had committed ourselves, a spirit of camaraderie rapidly developed among the members of the group. Although I had the job of providing leadership for the group, I didn't look at our times together as work. I began to look forward to our Thursday meetings as a time to spend with good friends.

One providential dimension of the group was the choice of Thursday as our meeting day. As the teaching pastor at Cherry Hills Community Church, my workload was heavily weighted on the front end of the week. I taught a Bible study for several hundred businessmen early on Tuesday mornings. Then, on Wednesday nights I taught another large Bible study. These events were emotionally, physically, and spiritually draining. By Thursday, I was usually shot!

Shortly after our Thursday group started to meet, I experienced serious emotional letdowns on Thursdays. I was also going through a period of discouragement in my ministry. Thursdays were becoming very difficult. I shared with our group the struggle I was going through. The men rallied to my side. They became a tremendous source of support as I worked though this time of difficulty. The group was rapidly developing all the qualities of authentic friendship:

1. We met together in a spirit of unconditional love to help each other grow spiritually.
2. We made ourselves available to each other and sought to be there for members of the group who were having a tough time.
3. We were learning to be open and honest with each other.
4. We held each other accountable for spiritual growth and lovingly, yet firmly, encouraged each other.
5. We met together regularly.
6. We prayed for each other.
7. We joked around and had fun together, too!
8. We were becoming authentic friends.

The point I want to make is that this was an intentional group. It didn't happen naturally. It was purposefully planned and aggressively pursued. The result was the creation of authentic friendships. If you are weak in the friendship area of your relational network, you have the ability to develop authentic friendships.

You might have an existing group of relationships that simply require a little work to develop into authentic friendships. Or there may be a group of men or women you have wanted to get to know better that could become a group like the one we started. You might need to be the "point person" who leads the way.

If you think you lack the raw material for such a group, I would recommend finding a good church to join. If you are already a member of a good church, there is probably a group right in your church that could become a covenant friendship group. If not, you might consider looking around for a church where you can find this caliber of fellowship. If you work on this component of relational priorities, you will soon discover your own Grace's Place where you can experience authentic friendship and find the encouragement and support you need.

Personal Reflection

The friendship factor provides another place to stop and take a look at the priorities of your life. As you think about the following questions consider making the necessary adjustments. Doing so could build this area of your life into another vehicle through which your needs for love and meaning can be met more fully.

- Who is the best friend you have ever had?
- Do you have a Grace's Place in your life?
- Are any of your friendships unconditional?
- Do you have a friend with whom you can be open and honest?
- Would you like to be held accountable in your spiritual life?
- Pray that God would give you a few authentic friends.
- Take action to start a small group.

CHAPTER TEN

Transcending Nonconformity

(Turn off, Tune out, and Drop in!)

The summer of 2019 marked the fiftieth anniversary of one of the most iconic events of our times. In the summer of 1969, a half-million young Americans gathered on a farm in upstate New York for three days of "love, peace, and music." The original Woodstock has become legendary. On August 13 and 14, 1994, a group of aging baby boomer entrepreneurs attempted to re-create the "magic."

This time, nearly three hundred thousand members of Generation X (and a few ex-hippies) worked hard, with a great deal of apparent success, to capture the spirit of the sixties. That decade was a period in which multitudes of searching adolescents harkened to the call of Timothy Leary and "turned on, tuned in, and dropped out" in an attempt to make life meaningful. The music at Woodstock was exceptional. The event was something of a mess. Let's face it; you can only stay high on drugs and alcohol so long while sliding half naked through the mud imagining that you've just found Nirvana.

Woodstock ended; Nirvana was not attained. The optimism of the sixties led to the cynicism of the seventies and the apathy of the eighties. Nonconformity was not the answer. Ironically, peace and love are exactly what we need to live full and healthy lives. They are not to be found, however, in substance abuse, casual sex, or even rock and roll. Paradoxically, these needs are only met as we leave behind a self-centered lifestyle and begin to practice self-extension through acts of service. This requires a relational commitment to the priority of our fellowman. This becomes the final rung on our relational ladder, and our final priority in the blueprint.

In 1979, Bob Dylan released an album entitled, *Slow Train Coming*. One of the songs on that album reminded the listener, "You've got to serve somebody" and specified, "It might be the Devil, or it might be the Lord, but you've got to serve somebody." We might not agree with every point in Mr. Zimmerman's theology, but the primary message of the song is indisputable. Life is about serving. The object of our service and the product of our serving will, to a great extent, determine whether our lives are fulfilled and significant or shallow and meaningless.

Who is the happiest person on the planet? Who is the most joyful person in the world? At one time, it could have been a very ordinary Albanian nun living in the slums of Calcutta. Agnes Bojaxhiu grew up in a comfortable home in Skopje, Albania.

Those who knew her well during those days uniformly report there was nothing exceptional about her. At the age of twelve, she began to sense the call of God. In 1928, at the age of eighteen, Agnes joined the Order of the Loreto Sisters and adopted the new name Sister Mary Teresa. In December of that year, she sailed for India. Eventually, Sister Teresa became a geography and history teacher at St. Mary's school for girls in Calcutta.

St. Mary's was located on a spacious and elegant piece of property, separated from the slums of Calcutta by high walls. In 1935, Sister Teresa began to regularly leave the walled security of St. Mary's to walk through the streets of Calcutta on her way to a second teaching assignment in the city. Those walks brought her into contact with the desperate plight of the poor in Calcutta. Eventually, she would receive what she refers to as her "call within a call" to the poorest of the poor.

It is impossible for most of us to imagine what Mother Teresa saw on the streets of Calcutta. She saw unwanted babies abandoned on the street. She saw men and women literally rotting to death from leprosy. She saw the elderly left to die in the gutter. But she saw more than human suffering. In her own words, as I mentioned previously, she saw "Jesus in a distressing disguise." For over sixty years, Mother Teresa responded to the call to leave the security of the convent behind to live and serve in the slums. She learned the secret of serving her fellowman without expecting anything in return. (On a side note, recent studies of her private papers revealed she spent the last forty years of this service with virtually no sense of God's presence.) What did this life of self-sacrificial loving and serving produce in her?

In 1969, British journalist Malcolm Muggeridge traveled to Calcutta to make a documentary on the work of the Missionaries of Charity firsthand. In his book, *Something Beautiful for God*, he describes how he discovered a remarkable group of women, living in the most meager circumstances, enveloped in an almost tangible atmosphere of joy.

Where do you find joy? It can never be acquired by the pursuit of physical pleasure. Joy is not a physical reality. It cannot even be attained by the quest for personal happiness. Happiness is a conditional emotional experience. True joy is experienced at a level far deeper than our emotions. Joy is a spiritual experience only God can create in the human heart. It is a product of his work of blessing in our lives. It has a direct relationship to our acts of serving our fellowman.

Shalom

"Make me an instrument of your peace." This was the consistent and persistent prayer of Saint Francis of Assisi. Growing up in a wealthy home in Assisi, Italy, Francesco enjoyed all the advantages of wealth. He lived to be served. A trip to Rome in 1205 served as the catalyst to a process of transformation in his life. He chose to respond to the call of God. Unlike the rich young ruler of Jesus' day, Francis renounced his worldly possessions and followed Christ in material poverty. His impoverishment led to spiritual prosperity. He spent the remainder of his life, like Jesus, seeking not to be served but to serve. (Mark 10:45)

The great passion of Saint Francis's life was to be an instrument of God's peace. In the Sermon on the Mount, Jesus taught the disciples, "Blessed are the peacemakers." (Matt. 5:9) The priority of serving one's fellowman provides a wonderful opportunity for experiencing something of the blessing and joy that both Mother Teresa and Saint Francis discovered.

Peacemaking is rooted in the Hebrew concept of peace. The Hebrew word for peace is *shalom*. *Shalom* was much more than a greeting in the world of the Old Testament. It was a word that captured the essence of what a relationship with God could bring to a life. Peace, in the biblical sense, has a much broader meaning than our limited use of this word. When we use the word *peace* we are often referring to the end of hostility. In the sixties, flashing two fingers in the air expressed the desire of a generation to see the war in Vietnam come to an end. It was called the "peace sign."

But *shalom* (although it includes the idea of the end of hostility) is a much more comprehensive concept. The experience of *shalom* in the Bible is intimately related to God's blessing. (Num. 6:22–27) *Shalom* was a multi-dimensional concept that included material prosperity, physical health, emotional contentedness, relational harmony, and spiritual salvation. *Shalom* is a state of total well being flowing from a proper relationship with God. It is a word that speaks of the quality of life all men and women long to experience. Our role in dispensing *shalom* is a critical component in living a life that meets our own deepest needs.

Heroes

A peacemaker is a *shalom*-maker. Because of the multi-dimensional nature of *shalom*, peacemaking encompasses a wide variety of possible activities. Peacemaking is an attempt to be an instrument of God's *shalom*. It requires that we "tune out" the cultural bombardment, which tells us to indulge ourselves and "tune in" to the needs of humanity. It means "dropping in" by using the physical, emotional, spiritual, relational, financial, and political resources at our disposal to improve the quality of another human being's life. Peacemaking is a tangible expression of loving our neighbor.

Becoming a peacemaker requires a fundamental shift in our value systems. Our cultural paradigm indoctrinates us with a subconscious message to "love things, use people." If we are going to get serious about the priority of relationships, we must experience a paradigm shift that motivates us to "love people, use things." This is the underlying philosophical value system of the fellowman rung on the ladder. It is the life philosophy of a peacemaker.

Peacemaking can take many different forms. Some of us have the ability to be physical peacemakers. By that I mean we can use our time, energy, and resources to improve the physical quality of another person's life. Others among us are better equipped to be emotional peacemakers. We all have the potential to be used by God to be spiritual peacemakers. God has uniquely created each of us to play a peacemaking role in our world.

Peacemakers are often the unsung heroes of our world. Maxine Jones was one of my heroes. During my years at Cherry Hills Community Church, she ran a ministry called Manna. The church was originally located in the wealthy Cherry Hills area bordering the city of Denver. It would have been easy for such a church to forget about the needs of the poor, but Maxine made sure that didn't happen. On Tuesday evenings, Manna Ministries opened its doors. Originally started by Maxine as a food bank, Manna eventually offered food, clothing, medical care, and even free haircuts to families in South Denver who were in need of a little physical *shalom*.

Sometimes, the needs of our fellowman require more than physical peacemaking. Dale and Alice Hudson are two more of my heroes. For decades, Dale and Alice opened their home to foster children. Multitudes of children have found a temporary home with the Hudsons. Sensitized to the needs of handicapped children through their daughter Dusty's struggle with cerebral palsy, many of the Hudson's "kids" had unique needs, which others were unwilling to deal with. Not only did Dale and Alice provide a physical home, they loved and nurtured these children emotionally as well. Miracles happened in the Hudson home. A few "hopeless cases" graduated from college and are living productive lives because the Hudsons have been dispensers of emotional *shalom*.

Rich Beach is another of my heroes. For over forty years, I watched a nearly endless stream of spiritually destitute men and women find new meaning in life through Rich's efforts in the area of spiritual peacemaking. I know, because I am one of them! With a winsome personality and genuine concern, it was usually only a matter of minutes into almost any conversation before Rich raised the question of a person's spiritual condition. His sensitive boldness opened a multitude of doors. Where need and openness were present, Rich tastefully shared how to have a relationship with Jesus Christ. In restaurants, on airplanes, at shopping centers, and in nearly every imaginable arena of life, Rich led people to Christ. The deepest spiritual needs of men and women were brought in touch with the *shalom* of God.

Walt Allmand is one of my heroes. Walt was a successful businessman whose Maxi Lights can still be seen on construction sites around the country and even around the world. In the early years of his business life, Walt struck a "deal" with God. Instead of living on ninety percent of his income and giving ten percent to God's kingdom, Walt decided to live on the ten and give away the ninety! He and his wife lived in a small house and he drove an old four-door Chevy. Massive amounts of spiritual, physical, and emotional needs were met in the lives of people around the world because Walt was a peacemaker. Today, his sons, Roger and Steve, and his grandsons, Brad and Bart, carry on that legacy.

One of my greatest heroes is also one of my life-long friends. I don't know of any greater peacemaker than my friend Bo Mitchell. He has launched so many peacemaking ventures that I wouldn't know where to begin to list or explain them. As chaplain of both the Denver Nuggets and the Colorado Rockies, he has been a spiritual peacemaker to hundreds of professional athletes over the years. He almost single handedly is responsible for helping plant two of the most successful churches in the Denver area where thousands of people have been touched by God.

As an emotional peacemaker, Bo has created and launched multiple ministries to meet the emotional needs of men and women. With a heart sensitized to the immense burden of parents and others who have become full-time caregivers, he created Game Day Memories. The organization provides an evening of respite for these heroes by hosting them at professional basketball and baseball games. What started in Denver has now spread to other cities around the country and continues to grow every year.

As a physical peacemaker, he has blessed so many men and women that again, I could never do the subject justice. Through Crosswalk Fellowship he makes sure a group of inner city pastors (his heroes!) always have a great Christmas by providing them with a very generous Christmas "bonus" every year. When I faced the incredible expense of providing for my wife's memory care, he is the one who put together a group of men and asked each to help financially to ease the burden, as I explained earlier. He is one of the most remarkable men on the planet and very few people know all he has done.

These are the real heroes of our world. They are the hidden saints, ones who improve the quality of life on our planet for countless multitudes. They are the peacemakers. Most of them are not much different than you and me. They have limited time and resources. Their weeks contain only seven days. Their mortgages are due on the first of the month. Their cars break down and their children need braces. So how do they do it? The answer lies in understanding that inside the belief system of every peacemaker, you will find a commitment to the priority of his or her relationship with his or her fellowman.

Becoming a Hero

I have not shared the preceding illustrations in the hope you would admire these men and women from afar. I have shared these stories to challenge you to become a peacemaker. Yes, you! You were designed and created to be an instrument of *shalom* in the life of your fellowman.

The Chinese character for the word *crisis* is a combination of two other Chinese characters. One is the character for *danger*, and the other is the character for *opportunity*. Our world is in a state of crisis. Our nation is in a state of crisis. Our cities are in crisis, our neighborhoods are in crisis, and often, our own families are in crisis. We are surrounded by crisis. But with the danger of crisis comes the opportunities crisis creates for peacemaking.

Never in human history have there been more opportunities to serve our fellowman. The danger most of us face is in becoming so overwhelmed by the scope of the need that we do nothing. In order to become effective as peacemakers, we need to sort through the multitude of opportunities available to us and focus our limited time, energy, and resources in areas where we can make our greatest peacemaking contribution. It is not enough to "visualize world peace." Living our lives with relational priorities requires us to become proactive in the peacemaking process.

If we go back to our diagram of the human motivational system we will see that out of our belief systems, we set goals and take action. We do this every day in other areas of our lives. You probably have certain financial goals for your business and family. To achieve those goals, you have pursued a career. In some cases, that career took years of preparation. Five or six days a week you roll out of bed and head to work. You act to achieve your goals.

Now you have a new goal. You want to serve your fellowman. At first this will be a broad goal. It will require that you treat people differently. It should affect the way you treat the people you live with, the people you work with, and the people you encounter throughout the day. Instead of viewing them as objects placed on the planet just to meet your needs and serve you, you begin to experience a paradigm shift. You look at them and seek to determine what their needs are and how you can serve them.

At times, this process is quite obvious. Disaster strikes an African nation. The media gives the event headline attention and dramatic coverage. You see "Jesus in a distressing disguise" of hunger and poverty. Your heart is moved to compassion. You feel like you should do something. In the past, you let this feeling fade without responding. Now it is different. You find an agency that is responding to the need in the name of Christ and write a check.

At other times, the appropriate response is more complex. You are sitting in church and you hear about a great need for Sunday school teachers. You feel stirred and wonder if you should sign up. In the past, you just ignored such pleas, confident that someone else would do it. How do you sort through the multitude of such situations you encounter? How do you discern the need from the call? Here are a few practical steps you can take.

Discovering Your Gifts

The call to serve is not intended to be a call to attempt something you cannot do. It is intended to be a response to a task you have been custom-equipped to accomplish. When you made Decision One in Chapter Six, many wonderful transactions took place in your life. You were invaded! Christ came to live in you by means of the person of the Holy Spirit. When the Holy Spirit invaded your life, he endowed you with supernatural abilities the Bible calls spiritual gifts. The Bible says, "But to each of us, gifts were given just as he willed." (1 Cor. 12:11, author's own translation). The spiritual gifts God has given us enable us to effectively accomplish the tasks we are intended to accomplish.

Identifying Your Passion

Without going into great detail about how to discover your gifts, a second dynamic of deciding where to invest your serving energy is understanding that God gives us a passion for what he has created us to accomplish. Our passion is intimately related to our person. Like snowflakes, no two people on the planet are identical. Every man and woman is an expression of the creative genius of God. We might warp and distort the beauty, but each person's uniqueness remains intact. God has providentially been involved in the development of your physical body, your personality, and your life experience. All these factors work together to create your passion. Certain needs and opportunities you encounter will "push your button" more than others. These signals are important. They are part of how God leads you.

Discerning Your Call

No dynamic of serving our fellowman is more complex and yet more simple than discerning the call of God. If you have never sensed God's call on your life, it would be extremely complex to attempt to describe this phenomenon to you. Once you have experienced a sense of call, the phenomenon is so simple it requires no explanation.

At times, God actually gives a call to service in an audible voice. This was true of the prophet Samuel at the time of Eli (1 Sam. 3:1–10). Usually, the call is not audible but internal. God engineers the circumstances of your life in such a way that you are exposed to the need that will become your call. Having been exposed to the need, you begin to have an inner stirring to see something done about the situation. That inner stirring grows in your life. You sense you are the one to do something. Somewhere deep inside, you just know God is prompting you. Someone has said there are some things you just "know in your knower."

When the call fits with your passion and spiritual gifts, you can trust that you've found a place in which to explore serving your fellowman. You then take action in the special arena God has designed for you. The Bible says we are God's "workmanship," and we have been created to accomplish "good works which God has prepared in advance for us to do." (Eph. 2:10)

What a great picture! God prepares the work of serving. God then designs and creates the servant. He endows the servant with the abilities required to accomplish the work and then creates a passion in the servant's heart to see the work done. God places a call on the man to do the work and empowers the peacemaking enterprise with the enabling ability of his Spirit. When properly understood, and experienced, serving is a no-lose proposition.

Don't be afraid to experiment. I have had to approach this subject conceptually, but in reality, the unique gifts and ministries God has designed for you to accomplish are often discovered in the laboratory of trial and error. Like the Nike commercial, the message in this area of the blueprint is "Just Do It!" Get involved. Find a place that fits your gifts, personality, and passion, and begin to serve.

The result of these attempts will often be a sense of God's blessing in your life. It is a powerful experience to see how God can use your life to improve the quality of another person's life. Hopefully this act of serving will lead to others. Your peacemaking efforts will begin to give your life a new sense of purpose. You will begin to be a hero!

In an earlier chapter, we saw how our sense of personal fulfillment is intimately related to the twin needs of security and significance. By developing loving relationships with the people in our prioritized network, we will begin to build a source that meets our security needs. In turn, when we invest ourselves in acts of service to our fellowman our need for significance will be met in new and unexpected ways. Here is the paradox of giving our lives away for the sake of Christ. In losing our lives for Christ's sake, our own deepest needs are met. We begin to discover the secret of lasting joy, which Jesus came to model and teach. We put together a relational paradigm that keeps our lives from taking a trip down the Boulevard of Broken Dreams.

Dynamics of Human Motivation

By now, perhaps all these commitments and changes seem a bit overwhelming. Good! Does living this way seem impossible to you? Great! Does it all seem a bit unnatural? Let me assure you, it is! This is supernatural stuff; it requires a whole new source of ongoing enabling. If you're going to be a blessing, you need to be blessed. In the next chapter, you'll get a few tips on how to make that happen.

Personal Reflection

Here are a few questions to reflect on and actions to take to help put this priority into action:

- What are you doing in your life that gives you true joy?
- Do you love people, or do you love things?
- How could you become a peacemaker?
- What needs in your church or community capture your interest? Could those needs be a part of your passion?
- Ask God to make his call clear to you.
- Step out and begin to serve somewhere. Trust God to guide your journey of serving your fellowman.
- Look around. Don't overlook the obvious.

CHAPTER ELEVEN

Getting Wired!

(A Guide to Synthesis and Empowerment)

A life built around a set of relational priorities can be extremely rewarding and fulfilling. It also has the potential to be unbelievably frustrating and discouraging. Our desire to live a more significant life will be rooted in a mind-set filled with good intentions. Most people have good intentions. I have never known a groom who entered marriage with the desire to fail. I have never met a father who embarked on the adventure of family life with the intention of neglecting or abusing his children. Most of the men and women I have talked with over the years about relationships have indicated they would love to have healthy and vital friendships.

Yet marriages fail, families crumble, friendships disintegrate, and the desperate needs of humanity remain largely unaddressed.

At the same time, I do know men and women who have vital marriages, healthy families, meaningful friendships, and who are making a significant difference in the quality of life on the planet because of their selfless contribution of time, talent, and resources. The difference is not good intentions; it is often a matter of what I call synthesis and empowerment.

Synthesis is the product of a unifying principle or dynamic that ties all the areas of relationship together. Empowerment is the product of a source of enabling greater than ourselves. I know of only one adequate source of synthesis and empowerment that can make a lifestyle of relational priorities effective.

The Possible Impossibility

Several years ago, I had an unusual and profound experience of enlightenment. Late one afternoon, I was out on a walk to work out some of the frustrations of an exceptionally difficult day. I really don't remember the specifics of the day, but I do remember feeling like I had failed in the way I handled them. The more I stewed, the more frustrated I grew. Finally, I came to the conclusion that I was totally incompetent and inadequate to face life's demands.

As I walked along at an extremely brisk pace, I began to say to myself, "I can't, I can't, I can't, I can't, I can't." My thought patterns fell into rhythm with my step. Although at first this was something of a dismal conclusion to my ponderings, eventually I began to sense a certain liberty in the experience. Suddenly, the truth of what I was thinking came into focus. *I can't!* That's the bad news. That is also the good news.

After a time of walking in the "I can't" mode, I was reminded that living according to the divine design is always rooted in dependence on the empowering reality of the indwelling presence of Jesus Christ. In other words, I can't but he can! As this truth sank in, I began to change the internal message I was repeating in cadence with my step. Suddenly, I was walking along sub-vocally repeating, "He can, he can, he can, he can."

In a flash, I realized this little formula is the secret of empowerment: *"I can't, he can."* To a life of consistent spiritual and relational effectiveness, we must learn to live in dependence on the empowerment of Christ, made real in our experience by maintaining a vital relationship with him.

At the heart of this relationship is a radical transformation that takes place in the very core of our beings. Before making a decision such as Decision One of Chapter 6, we were dead spiritually. The Bible refers to this reality when it says, "You were dead in your sins and trespasses." (Eph. 2:1, author's own translation) The result of this reality is the warped way of living I have referred to as the Solomon Syndrome. The belief system and mind-set produced by this syndrome is the product of a personality developed apart from the influence and empowerment of the Spirit of God. After making Decision, One the Holy Spirit, absent before, is now present and dwelling in our inner beings. This is not only good news, this is great news!

When Christ makes us alive spiritually, he begins a process of transformation which theologians call sanctification. This process has everything to do with our human motivational system. There are several dimensions to this transformation process.

The Bible tells us we are transformed, in part, by a radical change in our thought patterns called, "the renewing of your mind." (Rom. 12:1–2) Our old understanding of our needs and how to get those needs met is slowly replaced with the truth of God's revealed will for our lives. At first this is only cognitive information being processed by that funny gray matter in our cranial cavity. Over time, as the Spirit of God works in us, these truths make the critical eighteen-inch journey from our heads to our hearts.

The second phase of the transformation process involves implementing these new realities into our lifestyles and behavior. At this point, we usually begin to experience another good news/bad news situation. A genuine attempt to live according to the priorities articulated in this book should prove to be extremely frustrating. That is the bad news. On the other hand, when we understand the concept of empowerment, we will begin to realize this frustration is also the good news.

Every once in a while, I have a conversation with someone who is new to the life of following Christ. When the individual shares this struggle, I say something like, "I have some good news and some bad news for you." I then go on to explain, "When you asked Jesus Christ to come into your life, he came. Jesus Christ is in you. That is the good news. The bad news is, *you* are still in you!"

The Bible refers to this reality as the struggle between the flesh (you in you) and the Spirit (Christ in you). It is normal to feel a bit schizophrenic. Every genuine, authentic, biblical, regenerate person has a "split personality." If you want a graphic illustration of what this looks like, go to the seventh and eighth chapters of the Book of Romans. Beginning in verse 14 of Chapter 7, the apostle Paul shares his own struggle with living the spiritual life. The first time I read, "I don't do the things I want to do and I keep on doing the things I don't want to do," I remember thinking, "Wow! Paul felt just like I do." In other words, Paul is saying, "I can't!"

Unfortunately, many men and women never get past Romans 7. At the end of the chapter, Paul gives up. Then comes Chapter 8. The entire eighth chapter is a discourse on living in dependence upon the indwelling power of the Holy Spirit. The message of the eighth chapter is "he can!" In these two chapters, we see the secret of living the impossible possibility. Only by means of the supernatural enabling of the indwelling Christ are we able to live according to the divine blueprint.

Blessed and Empowered

What is the purpose of our life? It is to love and to serve. In Chapter 8, we found the primary task of the father is to bless his children. I defined blessing as a touch of God, which brings empowerment and wholeness in a life. There is a sense in which this is synonymous with loving and serving. We love with the love of Christ. We serve in the spirit of Christ. Our love and service become tangible ways in which God touches other people's lives to meet their needs.

Several years ago, I taught a teacher training class for the Bethel Bible Series. The Bethel Series gives an overview of the Bible using pictures and key phrases. The phrase the Bethel Series chose to communicate the overall theme of the Bible as "Blessed to be a blessing." It is based on the covenant God made with Abraham, which is fulfilled in Christ. When we love and serve with the love and spirit of Christ, we become a source of God's blessing. Blessing is the greatest need of our lives.

When we are experiencing this touch of God on our lives we feel loved unconditionally and infinitely significant. Notice that before we are able to be vehicles of blessing, we need to be blessed. The reason we are not effective in blessing others is often because we are not being blessed ourselves; there is no blessed father to bless his children, there is no blessed husband to bless his wife, and there are no blessed friends to bless one another in authentic fellowship. There are not enough blessed servants to meet the desperate need for blessing our fellowman. We need to be touched by God in a very real way, one that creates this experience of blessing. It is this reality that empowers us to live a relationally based lifestyle effectively.

Synthesis

We have repeatedly seen that if we are going to live in conformity with the purposes of God, the highest priority relationship of life must be our relationship with God. He is our source of power. He is the source of blessing. Our objective needs to be lived in a way that keeps us in the flow of God's blessing. For this reason, our relationship with God occupies the highest rung on the ladder of relational priorities. The quality of every other relationship in the network will, to a great extent, be a product of the quality of our personal, spiritual vitality.

The relationships of the blueprint are interdependent. I have heard it said that if you really want to love your kids, love their mom. This statement reflects the fact that a higher priority marriage relationship will significantly impact the quality of the parent-child relationship. The prioritization of relationships within the paradigm reflects this reality. This principle can be illustrated by taking the pyramid and reconfiguring it into a series of concentric circles.

Notice that power and influence flow from the center outward. Reinforcement flows back to the center. The inner priorities determine the quality of the outer. The Christ relationship is central. It is the Christ relationship that empowers and influences every other relationship in the paradigm. Cultivating this relationship is of utmost importance if we are going to effectively live a spiritually centered lifestyle.

Synthesis and Empowerment
In the flow of God's blessings

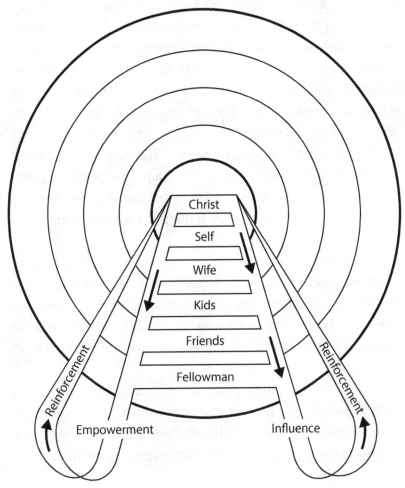

A Working Strategy

The walk I took at the end of my frustrating workday turned out to be a life-changing event. After the walk, I began to think about how I could keep myself in the "he can" mode with more consistency. I also wanted to figure out how to pass on to other people the truth I had discovered.

As I thought about this challenge, I was reminded of what a member of Alcoholics Anonymous once told me. I have always wondered why some men who join AA have tremendous results in their battle to overcome alcoholism while others seem unable to break the addiction. A friend told me the answer was simple. Joining AA is only one step in the recovery process. The real difference between recovery and ongoing disaster has to do with "working the program."

The genius of the AA approach to recovery is found in the "Twelve Step" program. The Twelve Steps give people a simple daily strategy for recovery. If you work the program, you will get better. If you don't, simply joining the organization will do you little good.

I immediately saw a direct analogy with the spiritual journey. What is the difference between the man or woman who breaks free from the Solomon Syndrome and the one who continues down the Boulevard of Broken Dreams? In many cases the answer is a matter of whether or not they have learned to "work the program."

I began to think through what a daily step-by-step working strategy might look like for men and women who were trying to put a spiritually based, relationally-prioritized lifestyle into practice. I came up with a seven-step program for daily spiritual vitality.

Step One

The first requirement for working through this strategy is to set your alarm to go off fifteen minutes earlier in the morning. Find a place to be alone and get a hot cup of coffee. Find a modern translation of the Bible and have a notebook and pen handy.

The strategy begins with the acknowledgment of our need. This is the *I can't* step. It requires that we remember and embrace the truth that apart from the indwelling of Jesus Christ and the enabling power of the Holy Spirit, we don't have the ability to keep off the Boulevard of Broken Dreams. Begin by telling God something like:

Lord, I am powerless. I can't be the kind of

person you want me to be today without

your grace and your help.

With that small acknowledgment, you will have taken the first step toward a meaningful and significant day. It is amazing how coming to grips with this reality first thing in the morning will help get your day going in the right direction.

Step Two

Immediately after acknowledging your inadequacy, take the second step in the strategy by affirming God's adequacy. This is the *he can step*. Again, in an attitude of prayer, tell God:

Father, you are all-powerful.

You have the ability to enable me to be the kind of

person and live the kind of life that pleases you today.

I find this affirmation is another great way to begin the day. It gets me thinking about how great God is and how much he loves me.

Step Three

The third step is the "plugging into the power" step. The experiential link in the entire spiritual enterprise is the indwelling of the person of the Holy Spirit. His activity in our lives enables us to do the things contained in the pages of this book. He needs to control, guide, and empower our day. Again, pray:

Holy Spirit, I ask you to fill my life

today with your presence and power.

Live the life of Christ in and through me today.

These three steps get us spiritually positioned to face the day in the power of the Spirit and live in a way we could never live without divine intervention.

Step Four

One of the dilemmas of living in relationship with God is the problem of free will. Wouldn't it be great if after you took the first three steps you could just go out and cruise through the day without any problems? Unfortunately, it doesn't work like that. Because you are a free, moral being, you have been vested with the ability to make bad choices at any moment.

When you take the first three steps, you have, in effect, dethroned self or ego from the control point of your life and enthroned Jesus Christ as Lord. The key to living with consistency, in the flow of God's plan, is maintaining this internal position (with Christ in control and ego in submission to the Spirit).

Step Four is a conscious step to invite Christ to reign as Lord over your life. It is as if you invite him to take control of the inner throne. This is a step that might need to be repeated periodically throughout the day as you become conscious that by an act of your free will, you have "bumped" him off the throne and usurped his position at the control center of your life. When you become aware that you have dethroned Christ, you need to stop and pray something like this:

> *Lord, I have done it again. I have dethroned*
>
> *you and taken control again. I willingly*
>
> *step down and invite you to once again*
>
> *reign as Lord of my life.*

Step Five

Steps Four and Five of the program are "in the heat of battle" steps. They will be helpful to review each morning so you will remember them when you need them.

Step Five is a step that often needs to be taken when you have usurped control again. Along with getting back into the right relationship with Christ at such times, you need to get honest with God and let him put his finger on things in your life that are out of conformity with his will. It is a step that appropriates the forgiveness and cleansing made possible by Jesus' atoning death and resurrection. When you become aware that you need this step, pray:

> *Search me, Lord, and show me where I'm*
>
> *off-track. I turn from my self-centered sin*
>
> *and ask you to forgive and cleanse me.*

Step Six

The sixth step in this daily strategy is a commitment to seek to grow in your relationship with Christ. You begin implementing this step the minute you set your alarm fifteen minutes early.

We have a variety of resources available to facilitate the vitality of our relationship with Christ. These resources are activated through the exercise of certain disciplines. The activation of the resources provides the empowerment necessary to live out the relational paradigm. All four resources and their corresponding disciplines have the object of getting us "plugged into" Christ in a dynamic way. If we use them as an end in and of themselves, they will become stagnant and unproductive. These are means to an end. The end is Christ himself.

Resource #1—The Bible

Communication is a critical component in every relationship. If we are to have an authentic relationship with God, we need to experience a special process of communication. Most communication begins with spoken words. God has spoken. He spoke through the prophets. He spoke through the apostles. He spoke through the incarnation of his Son. The message of the prophets, the apostles, and the Son has been recorded for us in the pages of the Bible. No other book in the entire world is like it. It is a "living and active" book. (Heb. 4:12) Through this book, God continues to speak. It is a powerful vehicle that plays a central role in our relationship with Chris

To have a vital, productive, and effective spiritual life, it is imperative that we develop a consistent time of interacting with the Bible. Again, our objective in spending time alone reading the Bible is to encounter God and allow him to speak to us. For many men and women, setting aside time every morning or evening to read and reflect on the Bible has proven to be an invaluable resource in cultivating their relationship with Christ. Over time, as this relationship matures, we will sense God communicating with us as we spend time reading his Word. As we seek to live according to God's priorities the Bible will become our manual for life, the blueprint for meaning and significance.

When I first began a relationship with Christ, I was skeptical about reading or studying the Bible. On several occasions in the past, I had picked up a King James Version of the Bible and started out on page one. It didn't take long before I found myself bogged down in some obscure genealogy. The book just didn't seem that exciting or relevant. After my encounter with Christ, I received two very good pieces of advice about the Bible that I will pass on to you.

First, I was encouraged to obtain a copy of a modern translation. If the King James Version seems archaic to you, it is because the King James Version is archaic. It was written in the language and style of England in 1611. Some men and women, who have been reading the Bible for years, love the "these" and "thous" of the King James Version. What many people don't understand is that this was simply the language of the common people at the time this version was translated.

If you are just beginning the adventure of cultivating a relationship with Christ, I think you will find that one of the many good modern translations will help immensely in getting started on the exciting journey of exploring the spiritual truths and principles contained in this book. I bet your pastor would be glad to help you choose a version, which you find readable and enjoyable. There are also many very good Internet sites that make various translations available. You might download the *YouVersion* app to your smart phone and explore a variety of versions to find one you like.

The second tip is this: start in the New Testament. Don't get me wrong; you will eventually find the Old Testament immensely helpful and quite fascinating. But to get off to a good start, begin by reading the New Testament. Start with one of the four Gospels. They contain the historical narratives of the life and teachings of Jesus. Try Matthew or Luke and then head on to John. Just a chapter a day will radically improve the quality of your inner life. Consider this a money back guarantee!

Set goals for yourself in this area. My personal goal is to spend a significant period of time reading and praying at least five days a week. These are often the best minutes of my day. All else is influenced by what happens in this time.

If you need help understanding the Bible, you might want to get a copy of my book, *The Word: A Guide to Understanding and Enjoying the Bible*. It is available on Amazon.com.

Resource #2—Prayer

Through reading, studying, and internalizing the Bible, God will begin to speak to us and transform our belief systems. But communication is a two-way process. We also need to speak to God. Through prayer we have been given this privilege. Along with time spent in the Bible, time in prayer is an essential means of enhancing our relationship with Christ.

Prayer is a form of communication with God. In prayer, we move into a conscious experience of the presence of God. For many of us, this discipline of growing in our spiritual life does not come naturally. We need to learn how to enjoy a more meaningful experience of prayer. Like the disciples, we have the need to come to Jesus and ask him to teach us to pray. (Luke 11:1)

Jesus responded to the disciples' request by giving them a sevenfold pattern of prayer. Most of us are familiar with the Lord's Prayer as a rote, memorized, and liturgical prayer. When used as an outline of seven topics, however, the prayer provides a helpful guide toward developing a more meaningful prayer life. I have dealt with this subject in depth in my book, *Prayer: A Strategy Based on the Teaching of Jesus.* It is also available on Amazon. For our purposes, let us briefly explore the seven components:

1. "Father" (*Relationship*)

Begin your time of prayer focusing on God as your heavenly Father and consciously entering his presence.

2. "Hallowed be your name" (*Worship*)

Prayer is a time to set our minds and hearts on the nature of God and give him praise and thanksgiving for who he is and what he does. Thank God for something he has done for you recently and praise him for some characteristic of his nature.

3. "Your kingdom come . . ." (*Intervention*)

In prayer, we have been given the privilege of appropriating God's intervention in our lives. Pray that the realities of his kingdom will influence your personal life, your family, your church, your nation, and the needs of the world.

4. "Give us this day . . ." (*Provision*)

With Christ as our highest priority we are able to pray with confidence for God's provision in our lives. During prayer, set before the Father your needs, your desires, and all sources of anxiety in your life.

5. "Forgive us our sins . . ." (*Forgiveness*)

Prayer is a time of getting honest with God. It is a time to wrestle with our flaws and failures and allow the grace of God to touch our lives with the cleansing work of Christ. Take a fearless moral inventory of your life and get back on track with God's will and his plans.

6. "Lead us not ... deliver us ..." (*Protection*)

Living a spiritual life is a battle. We need protection from our own susceptibility to temptation and also from the hostile spiritual realities that seek to harm us. Appropriate the leading of the Spirit and the protection of the Father.

7. "Yours is the kingdom . . ." (*Affirmation*)

God doesn't need our affirmations, but we need to remind ourselves that he is in charge, not us. Close your time of prayer with a series of affirmations regarding God's sovereign authority over your life.

Over time, as you grow in your personal prayer experience, many other dimensions of prayer can be added to this pattern. This pattern is simply designed to help you begin to practice a discipline of prayer that will put you in touch with Christ on a daily basis.

Resource #3—Fellowship

The resources of the Bible and prayer are direct, vertical means of developing our relationship with God. But there are also horizontal resources that provide additional means of facilitating our spiritual growth. Fellowship encompasses all those relationships we enjoy with our fellow travelers on the spiritual journey.

Since I have already spent a great deal of time exploring this dimension of the divine design in Chapter 9, let me simply point out again how these relationships are interdependent. There is a synthesis that begins to take place when we operate from a spiritual and relational center. In fellowship, we experience the reality of Christ's love as it is expressed through tangible, human vehicles. Authentic fellowship enhances our relationship with Christ. Our relationship with Christ enhances our human fellowship. This is where synthesis begins to develop.

Resource #4—Ministry

The ministry resource rounds out the picture. Since Chapter 10 was dedicated exclusively to this subject, I will simply point out that ministry to our fellowman has several benefits. Not only does it benefit the person being served, it enhances our relationship with Christ. Often, we will feel that we have had more benefit from the act of service than the person being served!

With the centrality of Christ established and these four resources active in our lives, our relationships will begin to thrive. We will have access to the source of synthesis and power. Men and women who live with the ultimate priority of the Christ relationship, have found the secret of living a life characterized by meaning, purpose, power, fulfillment, and eternal significance. Why wouldn't you want to live like that? This leads logically to the final step.

Step Seven

The final step in the strategy is a commitment to seek to be a vehicle that Christ can use to influence the world for the sake of his kingdom. After spending these minutes getting plugged in to the person and power of Jesus Christ, you will want to get the rubber on the road. At this point in my own quiet time, I often simply pray, "Put me in, Coach!"

As I began to use these seven steps as my own working strategy, I became convinced that many men and women needed a simple tool like this to keep their days productive and spiritually vital. I'm now working on a book that will expand these seven steps and hopefully provide a guide to a more consistent and effective spiritual life. If this book has helped you, keep on the lookout for my next book.

I believe if you work on cultivating this priority of your personal relationship with God, everything we have explored together in this book will begin to come into focus in a wonderful and exciting new way in your life.

Personal Reflection

Your relationship with Christ is the most important area of your life, and you need to submit it to consistent assessment and adjustment. This relationship is one that I try to take a look at daily. As you seek to develop your relationship with Christ, here are a few questions on which to reflect and a few suggestions about actions you can take:

- What in your life is a source of synthesis and empowerment?
- Set aside fifteen minutes a day for five days this week to read a chapter in the Bible. Begin with the Gospel of Luke.
- Try using the seven components of the Lord's Prayer to pray five days this week.
- How does your marriage affect your children?
- How does your spiritual life affect your marriage?
- What keeps you from developing the basic disciplines?

CHAPTER TWELVE

Swords, Staffs, and Groundhogs

(The Secret to Finishing Well)

As the old adage goes, "All good things must come to an end." What is true of all good things certainly applies to life itself. For those who consider themselves to be in the prime of life, it is difficult to imagine that one day their lives on this earth will be over. At eighteen, we live like we are indestructible. At thirty, we begin to notice weird things happening to our bodies. By forty, time seems to pass by at an accelerated pace. When we hit midlife, our mortality and frailty come crashing in upon us in not-so-subtle ways. If we are lucky enough to live a full life, one day, we will be in the unique position of looking back at the years and making some kind of an appraisal of how they were spent.

Over the last forty-plus years, I have had the pleasure of being involved in the lives of many men and women who are making the transition from living according to the defective value system of contemporary culture to a life based on the priorities of the divine design. Twenty years ago, most of the people I worked with were young and at the beginning of their careers and family lives. Today, I spend a great deal of time with men and women who are either going through midlife transitions or heading into late adulthood. One of the consistent concerns I hear from these people is the desire to finish well.

How tragic to come to the later years of our life and find that the systems and approaches that served us well in our youth really don't work well in later life. Newspaper and television reports seem filled with the accounts of men and women who have *not* finished well. What does it take to come to the later stages of life and look back with a sense of satisfaction, knowing that your life has counted for something that is self-transcending?

The View from the Bridge

In recent years, behavioral scientists have given much attention to what has become known as adult life cycles. The forerunner of these recent studies was the work done by Erik Erikson at Harvard University in the late sixties. While working as Professor of Human Development at Harvard, Erikson published a book entitled, *Identity: Youth and Crisis*. In this work, Erikson attempted to map out the stages of human development from birth to death. He theorized eight successive stages of human development and identified the major tasks that needed to be accomplished during each of those eight stages. The possible outcomes of attempting to negotiate these tasks provided the titles for each of the stages. The eighth and final transition period Erikson labeled "Integrity vs. Despair." Erikson observed that men and women who reached this final stage of life tended to look back and make some assessment of their lives. This assessment produced one of two conclusions. Either they achieved a sense of what Erikson called integrity, or they developed a sense of what he called despair.

Erikson found that in order to achieve a sense of integrity, three tasks needed to be accomplished. First, he found that a sense of integrity seemed to be rooted in the development of a series of relationships that produced intimacy. Second, he found men and women needed a sense that through their lives, something of value was being passed on to the next generation; Erikson called this task "generativity." Finally, he found that integrity was a product of what he called ideological commitment, by which he meant living one's life on the basis of a meaningful value system.

If, on the other hand, a person's life was characterized by isolation rather than intimacy; and if instead of generativity, one sensed that nothing of value had been passed along to the next generation (what he called stagnation); and if, rather than ideological commitment, a man or woman lived with what Erikson called confusion of values, then the assessment would likely be one of despair. These observations, by the way, were not made in a religious context; they were the conclusions of an expert in the field of human development at one of our nation's leading universities.

Ten years after Erikson's book was published, a team of researchers from Yale University published *The Seasons of a*

Man's Life. Daniel Levinson headed the team and the project about which the book reported. This particular study focused on the adult life cycles of men. Taking an interdisciplinary approach, Levinson and his team identified three major periods of adulthood. The final period was called "late adulthood." Levinson observed that during this period, each person has an experience he called, "the view from the bridge." Like Erikson's final stage, this period was characterized by a time of appraisal in which men make some assessment of their lives. Levinson saw the goal of this assessment to be the discovery that one's life has been meaningful and valuable. According to Levinson, such an appraisal is necessary in order to face death with a sense of fulfillment. Levinson's findings were identical to Erikson's. Both were perfectly consistent with the blueprint for living contained within the divine design of God's revealed plan we have explored together in this book.

For those of us who are familiar with the main themes of the Bible, there is nothing new in the work of either Erikson or Levinson. Almost 3,500 years ago, a man by the name of Moses wrote, "Teach us to number our days aright, that we may gain a heart of wisdom." (Ps. 90:12) Moses understood the importance of living with a sense of perspective. He knew that one day, he would stand on the final "bridge" of life and look back. It seems as if Moses was praying that the view from the bridge would be good, and the final assessment would be one of integrity and fulfillment rather than one of despair. Nothing could be quite as tragic as to arrive at the end of our lives feeling this sense of despair and knowing there was no solution to our dilemma.

Images of Despair

After reading both Erikson and Levinson, I reflected on the lives of biblical characters who modeled integrity and despair. Perhaps no historical figure more personifies the tragedy of despair like King Saul. Saul was the first king of the United Kingdom of Israel. He was a man who got off to a great start. Chosen by God himself, Saul was anointed to be king by the prophet Samuel. The Bible tells us the Spirit of God came upon Saul, and he led the armies of Israel to great victories over its enemies. At the age of thirty, Saul was on track. Unfortunately, the rest of his biography is the story of one man's decline into despair.

Acting presumptuously, Saul violated God's guidance given through Samuel. As God began to withdraw his blessing from Saul, another man, by the name of David, appeared on the scene. Saul responded to David's growing popularity with intense jealousy. In fits of rage, Saul even tried to murder David. His attempts to rationalize his blatant disobedience were met with one of the great rebukes of biblical history when Samuel proclaimed, "To obey is better than sacrifice, and to heed is better than the fat of rams." (1 Sam. 15:22)

Finally, God revealed he was going to take the kingdom away from Saul. Saul experienced episodes of what modern psychiatry might diagnose as manic depression. In desperation, and with serious value confusion, Saul resorted to witchcraft and sorcery to find guidance.

The final scene of Saul's life was dismal. It can be found in the thirty-first chapter of 1 Samuel. Saul was now seventy years old. The army of Israel had been totally defeated by the army of the Philistines. Saul's sons lay dead around him. In total despair, Saul leaned on his own sword and committed suicide. He left nothing behind but a life characterized by isolation, stagnation, and a total confusion of values. The view from the bridge was bleak. He did not finish well!

Images of Integrity

In contrast, the Bible also contains many images of lives characterized by integrity. One such image is found in what at first glance might have been a life voted, "Most likely to finish in despair." Jacob didn't have a great start. Although he was the son of the patriarch Isaac and the grandson of Abraham, Jacob was a scoundrel from birth. He came out of the womb jockeying for position and trying to maneuver into the place his older brother rightly held as the firstborn. He manipulated his brother into selling his birthright for a bowl of soup and tricked his father into giving him the blessing reserved for the firstborn. Having thoroughly swindled his brother and father, he was forced to flee Canaan to save his life. This flight was the beginning of a pilgrimage for Jacob, which would eventually bring him back to Canaan a changed man.

Jacob fled to the home of his Uncle Laban, who was quite a scoundrel himself. Jacob was about to get a healthy dose of his own medicine. Laban had a daughter who was a real knockout. Her name was Rachel, and Jacob fell hard for her. He contracted with Laban to work seven years for the hand of Rachel in marriage. After seven years, the big day finally came. Jacob went into the dark tent to consummate the marriage. There was only one problem. The next morning, he found Rachel's sister, Leah, lying next to him instead of Rachel! Apparently, Leah wasn't quite as cute as Rachel. The nicest thing the Bible has to say about her is she had "weak eyes." Laban justified his actions and talked Jacob into another seven years of work to get the girl he wanted in the first place.

Through a series of similar experiences, God used the circumstances of Jacob's life to begin to change him. Finally, the day came when Jacob headed back home, hoping to be reconciled with his estranged brother. The climax of this journey, and of Jacob's life, took place when he reached the banks of the Jabbok river. (Genesis 32) Jacob sent his family, his servants, and all his flocks across the river while he stayed behind to do business with God. That night, Jacob wrestled with the Angel of the Lord. He refused to quit wrestling until he received God's blessing.

The prophet Hosea gives us an important insight into the nature of Jacob's wrestling. He tells us Jacob wept and begged for the angel's favor. (Hosea 12:4) Jacob's real struggle was not with God but with himself. God was wrestling with Jacob on Jacob's behalf. We are told the Angel of the Lord blessed Jacob, but he also wounded Jacob for life. Jacob's relationship with God was changed, and with it, the course of his life. The staff Jacob would need to walk would be a constant reminder of what God had done in his life and of his dependence on God to meet his needs. From that night forward, Jacob was a different man. He began to live his life on the basis of ideological commitment, instead of his old value confusion.

The final scene of Jacob's life should be a source of encouragement to those of us who find it easier to relate to a character like Jacob than to many of the other heroes of the Bible. When God changed Jacob's character, he also changed his name. *Jacob* became *Israel*. He was the father of twelve sons who became the heads of the twelve tribes of Israel. At the end of his life, we see Jacob being used to bless the Pharaoh of Egypt, his twelve sons, and even his grandsons. In the final moments of his life, Jacob "worshiped as he leaned on the top of his staff." (Heb. 11:21)

What a great picture of a life ending in integrity! He had served God, he had loved and been loved, and he left behind a godly heritage that would affect generations to come. The view from the bridge was good; he finished well!

These two men provide vivid images of the view from the final bridge of life—Jacob leaning on his staff and Saul leaning on his sword. One is an image of integrity, the other an image of despair. One man discovered how to live according to the divine blueprint; the other locked into the Solomon Syndrome and traveled down the Boulevard of Broken Dreams. How can we be sure we finish well, leaning on a staff instead of a sword?

The Bottom Line

In his book, *The Seven Habits of Highly Effective People*, Stephen Covey writes people who want to live in a way that counts need to cultivate the habit of beginning with the end in mind. He encourages the reader to imagine his own death and funeral, and even challenges him to write his own eulogy as given by a member of the family, a close friend, and a member of the community.

In a sense, he is encouraging the reader to project himself into the future and decide what he wants the view from the final bridge to look like. Once you know what you want the end to be, you can then begin to make the choices necessary to achieve that end.

One day, unless Jesus returns first, you and I are going to die. Ultimately, our eternal destiny depends on our relationship with Christ. If we have received Jesus Christ's gift of forgiveness, we do not need to fear judgment. But one day, we will have a personal assessment to make. It will be the self-evaluation of our lives. We will each have to face the final view from the bridge. On that day, I believe the questions we ask ourselves will be quite simple.

Question One

Our first assessment will be an evaluation of whether or not we have developed intimacy. "Have I loved and been loved?" will be the first question we will ask. "Have I loved and been loved by God and other people? Have I made relationships the priority of my life?"

Question Two

We will also evaluate what we are leaving behind. "Have I left a heritage?" will be the second question. We live in a time and culture that places a great deal of value on the practice of leaving an inheritance. Unfortunately, little emphasis is placed on the practice of leaving a heritage. Someone has said that the correct answer to the question, "What did he leave behind?" is "Everything!" In eternal terms, the answer to that question might tragically be "Nothing!" Are we building a godly heritage that conforms to the paradigm?

James Dobson tells the story of a woman who left a great heritage for her son. Dr. Dobson was doing rounds on the cancer floor of Children's Hospital in Los Angeles. During his rounds, he met a little five-year-old boy who was dying of lung cancer. In the words of Dr. Dobson, it doesn't get much worse than that! But that little boy had a mother who really loved him. Every day when Dr. Dobson went by the room, the boy's mom would be holding her little boy on her lap and singing to him to help ease his pain. One day as Dr. Dobson walked by the room, he heard the little boy talking about "hearing the bells." He concluded the little fellow must be hallucinating and close to the end.

Later that day when Jim ran into the boy's mother, he told her about the incident. The mother began to laugh good-naturedly and told Dr. Dobson her boy wasn't hallucinating. She told him she had taught her son that when it was time for him to die, Jesus would come to take him home, and he would know it was Jesus if he heard the bells of heaven ringing for him. "Those were the bells of heaven, not a hallucination," she said. Later that day, the little boy died in his mother's arms as she rocked him and sang to him. I don't know if this mother could have left her child much of an inheritance, but I promise you this: At five years of age, he already had a heritage that took him through the worst life had to dish out!

Question Three

The final question we will ask from the bridge is "Have I served God?" The image of the view from the bridge is profound. Death really is a bridge; it is the final bridge that leads to our eternal destiny. In that instant, nothing will be as important as the answer to the question, "Have I served God?"

The answer to the questions asked from the bridge will be the product of how well we have assessed and adjusted our priorities. Every small assessment is leading us to the big assessment of this final bridge.

Groundhog Day is another one of my favorite Bill Murray movies. If you haven't seen the film, the story revolves around Bill's character, an egocentric weatherman named Phil, waking up to find out that it is the same day as it was yesterday. Day after day after day, it is the same day. But Bill's character remembers everything that happened in the preceding days and uses this information when making decisions in the new day. The big idea of the film is what would you do if you could do it all over again, knowing what you know now?

Standing on the bridge in the twilight of their lives, many men and women will wish they could have just such a chance. In that moment, will we wish we could go back and do things differently? The problem, of course, is we can't go back; it is impossible. We can live our life any way we choose, but we can only live it once. We make the choice: integrity or despair.

God's desire for our lives is clear. He has planned for our integrity. He has given us a plan for living well. The relationships reflected in the Ladder of Love are the best he has to give. His plans and purposes are intended to enable us to develop a blueprint for happiness. If followed, they will help each of us live a meaningful and fulfilling life; they will lead us to a moment when we will cross the bridge into eternity to live forever in a perfect loving relationship with God. The view from the bridge will be good!

He Who Wins

Life is precious. Life is short. It is too short to spend years living in futile ways that will never meet the deep needs of our lives. The choice is ours: the defective paradigm of a fallen culture or the relational paradigm of a loving God, the Solomon Syndrome or the divine blueprint?

Have you ever seen the bumper sticker that says, "He who dies with the most toys wins?" That is the lie of the cultural paradigm. I used to have a T-shirt that had a much better "theology and geometry." The back of the shirt bore the motto, "He who dies with the most toys still dies!" How true!

I'll tell you who really wins. He who has a great relationship with God when he dies— that's who wins. He who has a rich and mature marriage, one that has weathered the storms of life and has survived the years, that's who wins. He who has a healthy and vital family because he made the tough choice time after time with his kids and determined it was worth the cost, that's who wins. He who is surrounded by a group of friends who love him and are willing to go to the wall for him, that's who wins. He whose life has been meaningful and significant because he learned how to escape the myopic land of self and to invest his time, energy, and resources improving the quality of life for his fellow human beings, that's who wins. These are the real issues of life.

These are the choices that determine the quality of our existence, now and forever. This is what God's plan for our lives is all about. It offers an alternative to the Solomon Syndrome, a set of values and priorities that are guaranteed to make you a winner in the biggest game of all: life.

Personal Reflection

As you come to the end of this book, I encourage you to spend some time reflecting on the major components of your relational network and assessing how well you are doing in building a life structure that will make you a winner. Here are several ideas to help you accomplish such an assessment:

- Go back and review the questions at the end of each chapter and review the suggested actions that accompany the questions.

- With one of the illustrations of the relational paradigm in front of you, evaluate which area of the network is your greatest strength and which area needs the most work.
- If you are married, ask your wife to assess your greatest area of strength and greatest area of need.
- In prayer, ask God to show you what you need to do to get your life more in harmony with divine priorities.
- Share what you are discovering with a friend. Consider giving a copy of this book to a friend and discuss it with him.
- Brainstorm a list of actions you need to take to get your priorities in order.
- Say "no" to at least one activity this week that takes you away from time with people in your personal paradigm.
- Continue to read good books related to all areas of relationship (that is, marriage, family, friendship, spirituality, etc.).
- Live a long, good, productive, meaningful, satisfying, and blessed life!
- Finish well!

Notes

Chapter One: Boulevard of Broken Dreams
   John Kennedy Toole, *A Confederacy of Dunces*. New York: Grove Press, Inc., 1980.

Chapter Two: Life's Too Short to Drive a Chevy
   John Denver, "Blow Up Your TV," from his album, *Aerie*, R.C.A. Records, 1971.

Chapter Three: The World According to Tripper Harrison
   Stephen R. Covey, *The Seven Habits of Highly Effective People*. New York: Simon and Schuster, 1989.
   Meatballs, Paramount Pictures, 1981.
   Douglas Adams, *The Hitchhiker's Guide to the Galaxy*. New York: Crown Publishers, 1980.

Chapter Four: We Are Who We Think Other People Think We Are
   Abraham H. Maslow, *Motivation and Personality*. New York: Van Nostrand Reinhold Co., 1954.
   Lawrence J. Crabb, Jr., *Effective Biblical Counseling*. Grand Rapids: Zondervan, 1977.

Robert H. Schuller, *Self Esteem: The New Reformation.* Waco: Word, 1982, pp. 33-35.

David A. Seamands, *Healing for Damaged Emotions.* Wheaton: Victor Books, 1981, p. 103.

Chapter Five: Buckets, Ladders, and Paradigm Shifts

Westminster Confession of Faith: Drafted by the Westminster Assembly, 1647. The Shorter Catechism: Question One.

Chapter Seven: Making Love Last

Tom Robbins, *Still Life with the Woodpecker.* New York: Bantam Books, 1980, p. 112.

"The Chemistry of Love," *Time*, February 15, 1993.

John Cougar Mellencamp, "Jack and Diane," from his album *American Fool*, Riva Records, 1982.

Malcolm Muggeridge, *Something Beautiful for God.* New York: Harper and Row, 1971.

Chapter Eight: Buy a Harley!

Gary Smalley and John Trent, *The Blessing.* Nashville: Thomas Nelson, 1986.

Edith Schaeffer, *What Is a Family?* Grand Rapids: Fleming H. Revell, 1975.

"The Origins of Alienation," *Scientific American*, August 1974.

The Family Gone Wild is available through your local Christian bookstore for rental.

Smalley, p. 49.

Ross Campbell, *How to Really Love Your Child.* Wheaton: Victor Books, 1977.

Chapter Nine: Hanging Out at Grace's Place

Louis Evans Jr., *Creative Love*. Grand Rapids: Fleming H. Revell, 1977.

For more information see my small booklet, *Accountability Among Men*, published by NavPress, 1994.

For a discussion of the urgent versus the important see Charles Hummel's booklet, *Tyranny of the Urgent*.

For more help in the area of developing your prayer life see my book, *Prayer: A strategy based on the teaching of Jesus*. Available on Amazon.com.

Chapter Ten: Transcending Nonconformity

Bob Dylan, "You Gotta Serve Somebody," from his album *Slow Train Coming*, Sony Records, 1979.

Muggeridge, op. cit.

Chapter Eleven: Getting Wired!

Bob Beltz, *The Word: A Guide to Understanding and Enjoying the Bible*. Create Space Publishing, 2015.

Bob Beltz, *Prayer: A strategy based on the teaching of Jesus*. Create Space Publishing, 2018.

Chapter Twelve: Swords, Staffs, and Peggy Sue

Erik H. Erikson, *Identity: Youth and Crisis*. New York: W. Norton and Co., 1968.

Daniel J. Levinson, *The Seasons of a Man's Life*. New York: Ballantine Books, 1978.

Covey, p. 95.

About the Author

Bob Beltz is a minister, teacher, author and film producer. As an ordained minister in the Evangelical Presbyterian Church, Bob was co-founder and then Teaching Pastor of Cherry Hills Community Church in Denver, and Senior Pastor of High Street Community Church in Santa Cruz, California. He currently serves as Pastor Emeritus of Highline Community Church in Greenwood Village, Colorado where he was Sr. Pastor for ten years.

Bob went to University of Missouri where he earned his bachelor's degree, then moved to Denver where he earned his master of arts and Doctor of Ministry degrees from Denver Seminary.

Bob is the President of the Telos Project, a not-for-profit corporation working to impact contemporary culture with biblical truth. In this capacity, he has helped develop, produce, and market films for the Anschutz Film Group, parent company of Walden Media (*The Lion, the Witch, and the Wardrobe, Prince Caspian, The Voyage of the Dawn Treader, Because of Winn-*

Dixie) and Bristol Bay Productions (*Ray, Sahara*). Bob was the Associate Producer of Crusader Entertainment's film *Joshua*, based on Joseph Girzone's best-selling novel, and helped develop and produce *Amazing Grace: the William Wilberforce Story*. Working with Mark Burnett and Roma Downey, Bob was the Associate Producer of the Emmy nominated *The Bible* Series on the History Channel, *AD: the Bible Continues* on NBC, and the movie *Son of God*. Bob is the author of seventeen books, including the best-selling *Daily Disciplines for the Christian Man* and the novels *Somewhere Fast* and *She Loves You*.

Website: www.bobbeltz.com